Studies in environmental pollution

The law relating to pollution

J. McLoughlin, LL.M.

of Gray's Inn, Barrister at law
Research Fellow, Pollution Research Unit
University of Manchester

The law relating to pollution

An introduction

Manchester University Press

© 1972 James McLoughlin

Published by the University of Manchester at
The University Press
316–324 Oxford Road, Manchester M13 9NR
ISBN 0 7190 0499 3

Made and printed in Great Britain by
William Clowes & Sons, Limited
London, Beccles and Colchester

316035

Studies in environmental pollution
General introduction

It is apparent that the recent growth in public concern over environmental pollution has not been matched by a corresponding increase in understanding about the form it takes, the sources from which it originates, its effects or the manner in which it is (or can be) controlled. In part this is a problem of communication and in part a problem of research technique and objective. Confronted by a large, uncharted territory, it is tempting to retreat into some small corner, applying the tools of one's discipline to an aspect of one environmental medium's problem.

However, waste creation and disposal, whether in gaseous, liquid, solid or noise form, is an interrelated problem. Similarly, the significance of scientific research into the damage effects of pollution or the technical methods of controlling it can only be established with reference to the type of society in which the pollution phenomenon occurs. Equally, the examination of appropriate pollution control levels and the administrative instruments by which these are achieved is a hollow exercise unless the necessary scientific backing is to hand. In short, a genuinely inter-disciplinary approach to the whole waste problem is ideally required.

It is considerations of this kind which have led to the introduction of this series and which have conditioned its form. It is intended for three types of reader. First, the academic specialist who is anxious to gain a wider understanding of environmental pollution, particularly from the standpoint of disciplines other than his own. Second, those who are engaged in a professional capacity, technical or administrative, in some aspect of pollution control. Finally, the more general reader, who, we hope, will be attracted by the thoroughness of treatment, achieved with the minimum of technical terminology.

There is, in the series, a deliberate intention to treat the subject matter in an objective manner but, in so doing, not to avoid contentious issues. Apart from the existence of conflicting evidence and interpretation on some important issues, there are also differences in view on the research methods by which knowledge will be advanced. These are important matters which require careful examination.

Finally, it should be clear that though the monographs in this series share the same broad purpose, the particular treatment in each is the responsibility of the author and is not necessarily accepted by other contributors in the series.

Norman Lee

Contents

Preface

Pollution control is not a series of unrelated problems concerning air, water, the sea, land dereliction and the like. It is a single problem concerning waste, which often may be disposed of in a number of different ways. It is a housekeeping problem. It faces both the nation and the international community.

Hitherto, most books on pollution control have each dealt with only a part of the whole problem—air pollution, for example, or controls over inland waters. My purpose in publishing this volume is to provide within the covers of a single book an outline of all the forms of pollution control used in this country, so that the reader can see just how the nation tries to keep its house clean and wholesome.

It started life as a working paper written for the benefit of my colleagues in the Pollution Research Unit of the University of Manchester. Mainly thanks to their encouragement, it has been enlarged into this present volume. I have been encouraged also in learning that no other book has pulled together the various forms of pollution control used by the United Kingdom.

I naturally owe a great deal to my colleagues in the Unit, Dr Norman Lee, Dr Peter Saunders, Dr Bahador Hacjoo, Mr Chris Wood and Mrs Alison Luker. They have contributed much in thought and ideas as well as valuable criticism. I wish to acknowledge also the helpful advice and comments of Dr Gillian White, Mr Bert Raisbeck and Mr Frank Shepherd.

J. McLoughlin
September 1971

Table of statutes

Table of regulations

Table of cases

List of abbreviations

A.A.	Alkali, etc, Works Regulation Act
C.A.A.	Clean Air Act
D.T.P.A.	Public Health (Drainage of Trade Premises Act)
I.M.C.O.	Intergovernmental Maritime Consultative Organisation
L.G.A.	Local Government Act
N.A.A.	Noise Abatement Act
N.I.A.	Nuclear Installation Act
O.N.W.A.	Oil in Navigable Waters Act
P.H.A.	Public Health Act
P.O.P.A.	Prevention of Oil Pollution Act
R.P.P.A.	Rivers (Prevention of Pollution) Act
R.S.A.	Radioactive Substances Act
R.T.A.	Road Traffic Act
S.F.R.A.	Sea Fisheries Regulation Act
T.C.P.A.	Town and Country Planning Act
W.A.	Water Act
W.R.A.	Water Resources Act
W.W.C.A.	Waterworks Clauses Act

1   The pollution problem

It is possible to define 'pollution of the environment' in many different ways, to include many different forms of unwanted interference with man's surroundings. For the purpose of this volume, pollution is defined as

The introduction[1] by man[2] into any part of the environment[3] of waste matter or surplus energy, which so changes the environment as directly or indirectly[4] adversely to affect[5] the opportunity of men to use or enjoy it[6].

Notes on the definition

1 *'The introduction ... into ...'*   Pollution involves the introduction into some part of the environment of matter or energy. Contrast conservation, which prevents the destruction or withdrawal of some part or feature of the environment, or some of man's natural resources. Since pollution can result in destruction there is a large overlap of conservation and pollution control.

2 *'... by man ...'*   The environment has often been changed to the detriment of man by natural causes such as volcanoes or the depredations of animals. We are concerned here only with the effect of man's activities on his neighbours.

3 *'... into any part of the environment ...'*   When a mining company excavates and leaves considerable heaps of spoil on the surface, this is merely a redistribution of natural substances in their original form. There is no introduction of any new material or energy into the environment as a whole. Yet it comes within the definition of pollution: in the view of men outside the company, visual amenity in a particular area has been adversely affected.

4 '... *directly or indirectly* ...' The effect may be direct, as when it affects a man's respiration or despoils a pleasant outlook. It may be indirect, for example by destroying some form of marine life which is essential food for an animal of popular or scientific interest. When that animal is also a pest to farmers or fishermen, for example the grey seal, we must recognise that what is regarded as pollution by one may be welcomed as a benefit by another.

5 '... *adversely to affect* ...' Since we are concerned with man's opportunity to use or enjoy his environment, this is necessarily a subjective test. 'Pop music' from a transistor may be pleasure for one but pollution for another. But that other may change his attitude when the hitherto 'infernal machine' switches to a test match commentary. Poison which kills birds may be pollution to the ornithologist but a benefit to the horticulturalist.

6 '... *opportunity to use or enjoy it.*' This takes into account not only damage to a man's health or his property, but also his opportunity to find recreation and pleasure in his natural surroundings. A deposit of waste which changes the landscape and spoils the beauty that man finds in it is thus a form of pollution. The opportunity may be present or prospective. Potential uses or enjoyment are therefore taken into account.

This definition of pollution is wide enough to include pollution of the environment within private premises. The protection of people who are invited or permitted to enter private premises, whether socially, on business or as employees, is provided for, however, by such statutes as the Occupiers' Liability Act, 1957, Factories Act, 1961, and Offices, Shops and Railway Premises Act, 1963. Although admittedly a form of pollution, it does not come within the scope of this volume.

The waste matter and surplus energy to which we referred include: gases and particulates emitted to the atmosphere; liquid effluents discharged into fresh water, estuaries and the sea; solid wastes disposed of on land or into water; radioactive waste; heat, noise and vibration. They include substances such as pesticides which have been deposited to serve a useful purpose but which have left dangerous residues on crops, have been washed off into watercourses or have passed along food chains to affect higher animals.

The manner in which wastes are released into the environment is always a relevant consideration. There are many ways in which wastes or residues are dispersed so as to become harmless, as when they are discharged into the sea to be rendered harmless by dilution. There are also ways in which they accumulate in some area or some medium, in the way that radioactive tritium tends to accumulate in the hydrosphere and krypton in the atmosphere;[1] or become concentrated in some place, in the way that pollutants can concentrate in the tissues of filter-feeding molluscs or predatory animals. These problems of dispersal and concentration are difficult and highly technical. No attempt is made to deal with them here, but these tendencies must be borne in mind when considering the need for legislative control.

This volume deals only with present-day legal and administrative controls over pollution exercised in England and Wales. There are, of course, many other aspects of the same problem of disposal of wastes which are the concern of economists, biologists, physicians, planners and others. No attempt is made here to deal with these aspects of the problem, but the task of the administrator and lawyer must be seen in its proper context. Therefore it is relevant to look at the problem as a whole before examining the methods of control in any detail.

Both as individuals living in our homes and as members of an industrial and agricultural community, we each and all produce waste. If that waste can be disposed of without affecting others, no problem arises. As soon as the disposal does affect others, directly or by the most indirect route, we are faced with a social problem. The common law has been evolved to permit men to live together peaceably, permitting freedom of action but not permitting unreasonable interference with neighbours.[2] It does protect the individual from some direct and obvious forms of

1 See H. J. Dunster and B. F. Warner, *The Disposal of Noble Gas Fission Products from the Pre-processing of Nuclear Fuel*, UKAEA, 1970.
2 See the common law action of nuisance, page 8.

interference by pollution, such as excessive smoke or unreasonable noise, but for reasons we shall touch upon later it has failed to arrest the tendency of men to pollute the environment to the detriment of their neighbours.

There are also problems of control, arising from the task of disposing of waste on a large scale, which the common law was never designed to meet. The community must dispose of its sewage; it is also dependent on industry, which produces large volumes of waste. Many of the technical solutions to the problem of rendering these wastes harmless before releasing them to the environment are already known, but cannot yet be put into practice on a sufficiently large scale. Some are still prohibitively costly; others would throw a burden on rates and taxes, or on industrial costs, that we might not be willing to bear, remembering that industry faces competition not only at home but from factories abroad. The result is that we accept some degree of pollution of the environment and will doubtless continue to do so throughout the foreseeable future. The task facing us is to control it, to try to ensure that no unnecessary or disproportionate damage is done, and to see that no particular section of the population is called upon to bear an unfair share of the burden, whether that burden be in the form of damage suffered or costs borne.

This task of controlling pollution falls into three interrelated parts. One is to decide what degree of pollution to accept, or—to put it in a more attractive way—what standard of environmental quality we intend to maintain. In making this decision, there are many factors to be taken into account: the damage caused by the pollution, the benefits to be derived from the activity which produces it, the cost of alternative methods of production or waste control, the importance of the activity which produces the waste, the extent to which the polluter is able to bear further costs. And not only are costs and benefits to be balanced, but the rights of those who would suffer the damage are to be considered.

Another part of the task is to improve technical methods of waste control and disposal, so that higher standards may be achieved. A third is to enforce the standards which have been set.

In this country, standards of environmental quality are maintained by controlling the rates of emission or discharge of the polluting matter. To find a satisfactory balance between damage and benefits, which will give reasonable rates of emission or quality standards, is a complex task. It must involve in the first place an evaluation of damage, and in the second an economic analysis of costs and benefits. In practice, this will be an exercise too expensive in time and money to carry out in all fields of pollution control. At present those responsible for determining the permissible rates of emission are informed of the kinds of damage suffered; there is rarely a quantitative assessment and hardly ever an evaluation. The problems involved in this kind of work will be discussed in later volumes in this series.

At best, however, these evaluations and analyses can only assist the administrator. The final decision is inevitably and properly a political one. It follows that the decision-maker must remain accountable directly or indirectly to the public. The constitution of the authority which establishes these standards, and thereby determines the quality of the environment we are to enjoy, is therefore of first importance.

If a single standard is set for the whole nation, no difficulty is encountered in this respect; a Minister of the Crown can be given the authority and remain responsible to Parliament. Normally the demand will be for this same standard for all, but there are many circumstances in which a region or locality may wish to enjoy or consent to suffer a different standard.

The obvious example is the industrial area where the majority of people are willing to tolerate some pollution of rivers and dereliction of land in return for higher levels of employment and material prosperity. The effects of the resulting pollution may be entirely local, in which case, subject to satisfactory safeguards for individual and minority rights, there is reason for acceding to such local demands. Where regional or local standards are to be set, however, authorities which are responsible regionally or locally seem the most appropriate. Whenever these areas do not coincide with those of established local authorities, difficulties arise in devising the best constitution and adequate safeguards. These difficulties will be referred to in later sections, especially in that dealing with river authorities.[3]

3 See pp. 31 and 32.

The setting of standards cannot be divorced from the problem of enforcement: it is no use making laws which cannot be enforced. The control of noise presents perhaps the greatest problem, but great difficulties have also been encountered with litter and the discharge of oil at sea. In some cases the solution lies in better techniques of detection and means of proof. In others it lies in co-operation with industry, and in some sectors industry has readily co-operated. When the problem is particularly intractable, as with traffic noise, the best answer may lie not in direct legal controls but in good planning.

Town and country planners have in recent years been taking pollution into account more frequently in granting or withholding permissions. Planning is central to the control of most forms of pollution. Bad planning can aggravate pollution problems; on the other hand, good planning can reduce the effects of pollution, and even render legal controls unnecessary. No attempt is made in this volume to study the place of planning in pollution control, but no account of the law relating to pollution can be given without reference to the use of planning powers.

This is the context in which our legal and administrative controls are set. The remaining sections of this volume explain the relevant rules of common law, and outline constitutions of the controlling public authorities and their powers.

The division of this book into sections follows the pattern of existing legislation. This means that some sections deal with different media such as air and inland waters, but some deal with particular pollutants, as in the cases of noise and radioactivity.

There is an obvious convenience in setting out the law in this manner, but of course environmental pollution cannot be treated as a series of separate problems. Stringent control of air pollution can lead to an increase in tipping, and shortage of tipping space lead in turn to more sea dumping. This then resolves itself into a single problem of finding the method of disposal which offers the best combination of low cost and least damage. Furthermore, pollutants discharged to one medium often find their way into another. Discharges to air often fall out onto land or are washed into rivers; pesticides and fertilisers deposited on crops or land may be washed into rivers and thence to sea fisheries areas, or pass along a food chain to reach predatory animals and human beings.

There is obviously a need for close co-operation between existing pollution control authorities, and in some areas for a degree of overall co-ordination or control. This is much too large and complex a subject to be discussed in a short account of pollution control, but attention will be drawn to areas where lack of co-operation renders control less effective.

Finally, we must be constantly seeking improvement. Therefore one of the purposes of pollution control must be to maintain progress towards the ideal situation in which no damage is done. This will be achieved only after considerable efforts have been made in researching for and developing new products, new processes and new methods of treatment. In the face of strong pressure from the public some industries voluntarily undertake such work; others do so after pressure from the government; but in those cases where industry is reluctant, controls can be devised to compel the effort to be made, and even to direct it into particular fields.

Introduction to sections 2–8

The law relating to pollution derives from two principal sources. The first is the common law, developed by the courts through judicial precedent. On the one hand it has created criminal offences for which people may be punished; on the other it has sought to protect the legitimate interests of individuals by recognising legal rights which the courts will enforce on their behalf. The second source is statute law, with regulations and byelaws made under statutory powers.

Common law

At common law the only criminal offence committed merely by reason of polluting the environment is that of public nuisance. This includes any act which 'endangers the life, health, property or comfort of the public, or obstructs the public in the exercise or enjoyment of rights common to all Her Majesty's subjects'.[1] In theory this could cover many forms of pollution; in practice it is very little used.[2] It is certainly not a means by which any flexible form of control of pollution could be exercised.

Civil, as opposed to criminal, actions have been more common. For any such action to proceed there must be a plaintiff who can show that some right he is entitled to enjoy has been infringed by the defendant. In each section, therefore, it will be necessary first to determine which people have rights, and what those rights are. The remedies granted to the successful plaintiff are normally damages and/or injunction.

1   1 Hawkins c. 75.
2   P.H.A., 1936, now provides a special statutory procedure by which public nuisances can be dealt with by magistrates. Proceedings under this section have been fairly common. These are dealt with under the heading 'Statutory nuisances' in section 4, 'Air pollution'.

The fact that there must be a plaintiff whose legal rights have been transgressed and whose interests have been affected so substantially that he is willing to incur the risks and expenses of litigation means that the effect of these civil remedies is uncertain and sporadic. A brewery or a wealthy angling club may litigate, but not an ordinary resident. The introduction of legal aid seems to have given little or no impetus to the common law in this field. Furthermore the plaintiff may settle the dispute on terms which are satisfactory to himself and the defendant but not necessarily to others affected by the pollution, who have not joined in the action.

Statute law

Statutes passed for the purpose of preventing or reducing pollution usually seek to achieve this by creating offences, with penalties in the form of fine and imprisonment. In some cases these reinforce the common law where the existence of civil remedies has failed to check pollution; in other cases they go beyond the common law, creating new duties. Only in the field of nuclear energy and oil pollution at sea have they directly modified civil liability.

Whenever a statute imposes on a person a duty, and as a result of a breach of that duty another is injured, the question arises whether or not that other person has a right of action at civil law for breach of statutory duty. The mere fact the wrongdoer is subject to a penalty under the statute does not necessarily mean that he is not liable to compensate the person injured.[3] To answer the question one must look at each statute and ask whether or not Parliament intended to confer a right of action on individuals so injured. In many instances it clearly did not. For example, in the Rivers (Prevention of Pollution) Acts, 1951–61, offences are created for which proceedings can be taken only by a river authority or with the consent of the

3 The Factories Act, 1961, imposes penalties on employers. It is well established when an employee may sue for breach of statutory duty if his injury is the result of a contravention of its provisions.

Attorney-General.[4] In other instances the question may be more difficult to answer, but it is rarely raised, since there is nearly always a corresponding right of action at common law.

In each of the following sections the common law will first be examined, followed by an account of the relevant statutory provisions. No account will be taken of local Acts of Parliament, for although in boroughs some of the older provisions were far-reaching, they are little used today in pollution control.

4   See R.P.P.A., 1961, s. 11.

2   Inland waters

Common law

Right to abstract water

At common law a riparian owner had a right to abstract from
a stream all water necessary for ordinary purposes connected
with his riparian tenement, even though his action might have
completely exhausted the stream. Other landowners had rights
at common law to abstract from underground watercourses and
wells, and to collect water percolating through their land.
Statute has now so completely taken away those rights that
they no longer merit discussion. By the Water Resources Act,
1963, all abstractions of water are controlled by the river
authorities.

Right to receive water unpolluted

A landowner has no right to receive water which percolates
through the ground. Yet he has a right of action if pollutants
released by his neighbour foul the water he draws from wells on
his land.[1] Lindley L.J. expressed this clearly and forcibly when
he said,

> *prima facie* no man has a right to use his own land in such a way
> as to be a nuisance to his neighbour, and whether the nuisance is
> effected by sending filth on to his neighbour's land, or by putting
> poisonous matter on his own land and allowing it to escape on to
> his neighbour's land, or whether the nuisance is effected by poison-
> ing the air which his neighbour breathes, or the water which he
> drinks, appears to me to be wholly immaterial.[2]

If the water flows along a defined channel, whether on the

---

1   Ballard *v* Tomlinson (1885) 29 Ch.D. 115. See also Shaw *v* White-
    head (1884) 27 Ch.D. 588.
2   Ballard *v* Tomlinson (1885) 29 Ch.D. 115 at 126.

surface or underground,[3] the rights of the riparian owner go
further. In Embery v Owen[4] Parke B. said,

Flowing water is *publici juris*—not a *bona vacans* to which the first
occupant can acquire an exclusive right. It is public and common
in the sense that all who have the right of access to it may reasonably use it. The right and benefit of water flowing past his land is
not the absolute and exclusive right to all the flow of water in its
natural state, but a right only to the flow of water in its natural
state subject to the similar rights of all the riparian owners. Therefore for an unauthorised and unreasonable use of this common
benefit will an action lie. He has no property in the water itself,
but a simple usufruct as it passes along.

Parke B. was speaking then only of riparian owners, but others
who have interests that the law will protect are given similar
rights of action. These will normally be people who derive rights
from riparian owners, such as purchasers of fishing rights. They
form, however, a limited class of people.

As we have seen, statute now forbids any riparian owner to
make an unauthorised abstraction of water, and of course
authorises abstractions by statutory undertakings and others.
The riparian owner still retains his common law rights to use
the water for certain purposes connected with his tenement.[5]
Subject to authorised abstractions, therefore,

every riparian owner is thus entitled to the water of his stream, in
its natural flow, without sensible diminution or increase and without sensible alteration in its character or quality. Any invasion of
this right causing actual damage or calculated to found a claim
which might ripen into an adverse right[6] entitles the party injured
to the intervention of the court.[7]

The riparian owner therefore has a right of action against
any owner upstream and presumably against any other person
who pollutes the water of the stream, and can succeed without
being called upon to prove actual damage. His cause of action
lies in nuisance, and, if any solid matter is deposited on his

3   Chasemore v Richards (1859) 11 E.R. 140.
4   (1851) 155 E.R. 579.
5   See W.R.A., 1963, s. 24.
6   A right to commit what could otherwise be an actionable nuisance
    can be gained by twenty years' usage.
7   John Young v Bankier Distillery [1893] A.C. 691 at 698.

land, in trespass.[8] That this is still an effective remedy was shown by the case of Pride of Derby Angling Association *v* British Celanese and others.[9] The plaintiffs were the owners of a fishery in the Trent and Derwent, and a riparian owner: the defendants were British Celanese and BEA against whom the claim was based on thermal pollution, and Derby corporation for discharge of insufficiently treated sewage. The action was in nuisance. The main interest in the case lies in the liability of the local authority, despite the combined effect of the increased number of houses in the area, and the right of their owners to connect with the sewerage system. The relevant facts and findings of the case are as follows.

Derby corporation had constructed its sewerage system under powers granted by the Derby Corporation Act, 1901, and it was then effective to deal with the sewage of Derby without polluting the river Derwent. They later enlarged the system because the increase in the population of Derby had made it inadequate. Further increase in the population rendered the system once again inadequate. When sued over the resulting pollution, Derby corporation pleaded that it resulted from the increase in population, that this was a circumstance beyond their control, and that the pollution did not arise from any actionable negligence on their part. The court found it was a nuisance attributable to Derby corporation, and that it was neither expressly nor by implication authorised by statute. An injunction was granted but its operation suspended so as to allow time to construct enlarged sewage disposal works. The judgement of Denning L.J. is of particular interest. He did not accept that the growth in housing development was beyond the control of the corporation: he pointed out that local authorities are themselves substantial builders of premises, and also control other development through their planning powers.

Notwithstanding this decision of the Court of Appeal, in the following year Upjohn J. at first instance[10] found Ilford corporation not liable when, during periods of heavy rain, sewage

8   Jones *v* Llanrwst U.D.C. [1911] 1 Ch. 193. Note, however, the comments on nuisance in Section 4, 'Air pollution'.
9   [1953] Ch. 149.
10 Smeaton *v* Ilford Corporation [1954] Ch. 450.

erupted through a manhole and onto the plaintiff's land. He found that the flooding was caused by the overloading of the sewers after increased building in the area, and held that, since occupiers of the premises were entitled by law to connect with the corporation's sewers, the corporation had not caused, continued or adopted the nuisance. There are several unsatisfactory features about the Ilford decision. Whatever doubts may remain on points of law raised in the Pride of Derby case, that decision remains the most authoritative, and local authorities will ignore it at their peril.

A local authority is offered no protection from civil action by the Public Health Acts, for the Act of 1936 expressly provides:[11]

Nothing in this part of this Act[12] shall authorise any local Authority to construct or use any public or other sewer, or any drain or outfall, for the purpose of conveying foul water into any natural or artificial stream, watercourse, canal, pond or lake, until the water has been so treated as not to affect prejudicially the purity and quality of the water in the stream, watercourse, etc . . .

and, at s. 31,

A local authority shall so discharge functions under the foregoing provisions of this part of the Act as not to create a nuisance.

and s. 331 provides that:

Nothing in this Act shall authorise a local authority injuriously to affect any reservoir, canal, watercourse, river or stream, or any feeder thereof, or the supply, quality or fall of water contained on or in any feeder of, any reservoir, canal . . . etc . . . without the consent of any person who would, if the Act had not been passed, have been entitled by law to prevent, or be relieved against, the injurious affection of the supply, quality or fall of water contained in that reservoir, canal, etc.

There are dicta to support the view that it is no defence to prove that the stream was already so polluted by others that the discharge caused no actual damage. In Crossley *v* Lightowler[13] Lord Chelmsford L.C. said,

11 Section 30.
12 This part of the Act deals with sanitation and buildings.
13 (1866–67) 11 Ch. App. Cas. 478 at 481–2. See also Wood *v* Ward (1849) 154 E.R. 1047 at 1057.

Where there are many existing nuisances, either to the air or to water, it may be very difficult to trace to its source the injury occasioned by any one of them, but if the Defendants add to the former foul state of the water, and yet are not to be responsible on account of its previous condition, this consequence would follow, that if the Plaintiffs were to make terms with the other polluters of the stream so as to have water free from impurities produced by their works, the Defendants might say, 'We began to foul the stream at a time when, as against you, it was lawful to do so, inasmuch as it was unfit for your use, and you cannot now, by getting rid of the existing pollution from other sources, prevent our continuing to do what, at the time when we began, you had no right to object to'.

This statement is open to criticism. Once the discharge has become a nuisance, the plaintiff is debarred from preventing its continuance only if the defendant can show a prescriptive right. If previously it was lawful to discharge into the stream, that can hardly mature into a prescriptive right, for prescription is based on a presumption, arising from the evidence of long enjoyment, that at one time the owner actually granted a right.[14] The discharge, therefore, is not 'calculated to found a claim which might ripen into an adverse right',[15] entitling the plaintiff to the intervention of the court, until it is capable of doing present damage.

Nevertheless it seems sensible to permit a riparian owner to stop sources of pollution at the outset, even though their effects are for the time being obscured by other sources of more severe pollution. Otherwise he is faced with the difficult, expensive and uncertain task of identifying each pollutant in turn as an effective or potential cause of present damage.

In theory it is possible for the defendant to prove that as against the plaintiff he has acquired a prescriptive right to pollute the water. This he does by showing that he has discharged into the stream openly and as of right for twenty years without action having been taken by the plaintiff to prevent him. In

14 Gardner *v* Hodgson's Kingston Brewery [1903] A.C. 228 at 239. On the creation of easements by prescription see R. E. Megarry and H. W. R. Wade, *The Law of Real Property*, third edn, Stevens, London, 1966, pp. 837 *et seq*.
15 John Young *v* Bankier Distillery [1893] A.C. 691 at 698. For fuller quotation see p. 12.

Hulley *v* Silversprings Bleaching & Dyeing Co.[16] a claim to prescriptive right failed on each of three grounds: the discharge had not been made openly and as of right, there had been a change in both the point of discharge and the amount of pollutant emitted, and finally the discharge had been contrary to the Rivers (Pollution Prevention) Act, 1876, and there can be no prescriptive right to do something forbidden by statute. Today a discharge may no longer be an offence by reason of consent given by a river authority,[17] but it is doubtful if any factory or local authority would, after having gained such consent, continue to discharge for twenty years with no increase in quantity or change in quality of the effluent.

Other rights that the common law will protect are rights of navigation and fishing rights. In stretches of river which are tidal the public has a right to navigate and to take fish. In non-tidal parts of rivers a public right of navigation can be acquired, but it is limited to a right of passage; it does not entitle the public to fish. Individuals may be granted fishing rights by the owner, or they may acquire them by long usage, and local inhabitants may by local custom acquire the right to fish.

The common law, therefore, protects the rights of certain limited classes of people. Although effective remedies are provided by way of damages and injunction, this has obviously failed to check pollution. It is only rarely that there is a plaintiff whose interests are so severely affected that he will be willing to embark on litigation to protect them. Parliament, therefore, has long considered it necessary to impose some form of statutory control. These controls are found principally in the Rivers (Prevention of Pollution) Acts, 1951–61.

Statutory control

Control over the use of inland waters has been centred on the river authorities by the Water Resources Act, 1963. That Act both provided for the establishment of those authorities and set out their powers and duties. Their duties cover control over

16 [1922] 2 Ch. 268.
17 See p. 22.

abstraction of water from natural water resources within their areas, and control, inherited from the river boards, over the discharge of effluents into the river systems.

Section 4 sets out the duties of the river authorities in relation to water resources. Each authority is under a duty

to take action as they may from time to time consider necessary or expedient, or as they may be directed to take by virtue of this Act, for the purpose of conserving, redistributing or otherwise augmenting water resources[18] in their area, of securing the proper use of water resources in their area, or of transferring such resources to the area of another river authority.

They are given more specific duties as follows:

Section 14.   'To carry out a survey of water resources of their area and of existing demand ... and to prepare a report.

'To prepare an estimate of future demand ...'

'To formulate proposals as to action to be taken by the river authority ... for any of the purposes mentioned in s. 4.'

To keep the above matters under review, and to carry out revisions at intervals of not more than seven years

Section 15.   To submit a hydrometric scheme for obtaining measurements and particulars of rainfall, evaporation, flow level or volume and 'other matters appearing to the authority to affect or be likely to affect water resources in their area'.

Sections 19 and 20.   To consider for which inland waters minimum acceptable flows ought to be determined, and to submit to the Minister[19] a draft statement indicating in respect of such waters the control points, methods of measurement and minimum acceptable flows at these points.

To keep under review their statements of minimum acceptable flows.

Sections 23–35.   To grant licences to abstract water from

18 'Water resources' means all inland waters within their area, with the exception of lakes, ponds, etc, or groups of lakes, ponds, etc, which do not discharge into inland waters. See s. 2.
19 Now the Secretary of State for the Environment.

resources within their area. (For exceptions and persons entitled to licence as of right see the relevant sections.)

Powers to control the pollution of 'streams'[20] were transferred to them from the river boards, predecessors of the river authorities, by the Water Resources Act, 1963, s. 5. Further powers to control pollution of underground strata were added by ss. 72–5.

The river authorities are in turn subject to the control of the relevant Minister, who for the purposes of water resources and river pollution is the Minister for Local Government and Development.[21] Each year they must submit a report to the Minister, with copies to the Minister of Agriculture, Fisheries and Food and to their constituent councils. By s. 107 'the Minister may give the river authorities such directions as he considers expedient'. If he considers, after a local enquiry, that a river authority has failed to carry out any of its functions, he may declare it to be in default, and give directions for the performance of those functions.[22] In general, appeals lie from decisions of river authorities to the Minister,[23] with a limited right of appeal to the courts.[24]

Control of pollution of streams and underground strata

River authorities have overriding control over the pollution of inland waters, with the exception of lakes or ponds which do not discharge into other inland waters. Both the Rivers (Pollution Prevention) Act, 1951, and the Salmon and Freshwater Fisheries Act, 1923, make it an offence to pollute certain waters, while bye laws of local fisheries committees create other offences; yet

20 'Streams' includes any river, stream, watercourse or inland water whether (natural or artificial), except that it does not include any lake or pond which does not discharge to a stream or any sewer vested in a local authority, or any tidal waters (R.P.P.A., 1951. s. 11(1)). But see powers to extend jurisdiction to tidal waters and parts of the sea, p. 23.
21 Statutory powers are vested in the Secretary of State for the Environment, but day-to-day control is exercised by the Minister for Local Government and Development.
22 For details of these default powers see s. 108.
23 The Minister may establish a tribunal by which, in specified cases or classes of cases, appeals or references will be heard: s. 116.
24 Section 117.

a river authority can give consent to a polluting discharge, whereupon no offence is committed. Polluting discharges into underground strata, which would otherwise be unlawful, can be made with the consent of the river authority. Local authorities have a duty to receive domestic sewage from premises within their area, and may also agree to receive trade effluents, but can discharge into a stream only with the consent, once again, of the river authority. Thus river authority consents form the key to the system of control.[25]

Rivers (Prevention of Pollution) Acts, 1951–61

Basically it is an offence to cause or knowingly permit to enter any stream[26] any poisonous, noxious or polluting matter.[27] The Acts also provide that a local authority is deemed to cause or knowingly permit substances to enter the stream in cases where it is bound to receive those substances into its sewers, and also where it has consented to receive those substances.[28] The former case refers to the reception of domestic sewage, the latter to trade effluents. The persons so discharging into the sewers are not guilty of an offence.[29]

A person 'causes' a substance to enter a stream if he sets it in motion along a course which must take it there, even though it passes along a conduit vested in someone else.[30] Subject to s. 2(2), which protects persons discharging into local authority sewers or sewage disposal works, he may be guilty of an offence under the Act. The owner of the conduit would be guilty of knowingly permitting the discharge unless he did not know of it, or could not have prevented it.[31]

Where a person brings a substance to the banks of a stream and spillage occurs through no deliberate act on his part, the question of whether or not he 'caused' the pollution arises. This

25 See also 'Statutory water undertakers', pp. 36–49.
26 For the definition of stream for this purpose see note 18.
27 R.P.P.A., 1951, s. 2(1)(a).
28 R.P.P.A., 1951, s. 2(1).
29 R.P.P.A., 1951, s. 2(2).
30 Butterworth v West Riding of Yorkshire River Board [1909] A.C. 45.
31 Yorkshire West Riding Council v Holmfirth Urban Sewerage Authority [1894] 2 Q.B. 842.

question of causation has given rise to difficulty in this as in
other branches of English law. In Moses *v* Midland Railway[32]
the defendant railway company drew along a line running
parallel with a stream a tank wagon containing creosote. This
wagon was the property of a private owner, and was apparently
in fit condition when the company received it—there was no
latent defect which would have been discoverable by a normal
inspection carried out with reasonable care. As it travelled
along the line a signalman noticed that liquid was escaping from
it. He telephoned ahead, and the defect was found to be a leak-
ing tap which the guard immediately remedied; but unknown
to the company or its servants the creosote had drained into the
stream. The statement of case was consistent with the creosote
having reached the stream before the signalman saw it. Lord
Reading C.J. found that in these circumstances the railway
company was not guilty of causing it to flow into the stream.
He added that if the creosote had formed pools by the track
during the time the train was stopped for repair, and no
measures had been taken to prevent leakage into the stream,
that would have been a different case. Presumably the railway
company could have been guilty of knowingly permitting.

In the more recent case of Alphacell *v* Woodward[33] the
defendant firm had a settling-tank for effluent with pumps which
operated automatically to prevent untreated effluent from over-
flowing into the river. Due to an accumulation of leaves and
brambles the pumps failed to work properly, with the result
that the tank overflowed. Magistrates convicted them of causing
polluting matter to enter the river contrary to the Rivers (Prevention of Pollution) Act, 1951, s. 2(1). The Queen's Bench
Divisional Court dismissed the appeal, deciding the issue simply
on whether or not the company has 'caused' the matter to enter
the stream. There had been no finding of negligence.[34] Leave to
appeal to the House of Lords was granted, the question for
consideration being

Whether the offence of causing pollution matter to enter the stream
contrary to s. 2 can be committed by a person who has no know-

32 (1915) 84 L.J.K.B. 2181.
33 [1971] 2 All E.R. 910.
34 Bridge J. [1971] 2 All E.R. at 915.

ledge of the fact that polluting matter is entering the stream, and has not been negligent in any respect.

It seems clear that a person may be guilty even though he has no knowledge of the polluting matter entering the stream, for the section reads 'causes or knowingly permits'. By implication it does not mean 'knowingly causes'. It has also been established that he may be found innocent if the spillage followed from the act of a third party, at least if that act was not a natural consequence of the defendant's conduct.[35] Where the intervening event is a natural development, such as the growth of vegetation, and not involving the interposition of another independent will, the court is unlikely to find that the defendant himself has not caused the spillage. Widgery L.J.[36] quoted with approval the dictum of Coke J. in Impress (Worcester) v Rees,[37] where he said that the question is 'whether that intervening cause was of so powerful a nature that the conduct of the appellants was not a cause at all but was merely part of the surrounding circumstances'. The question certainly is one of causation, not foreseeability, and it is difficult to see how negligence is relevant.

The decision of the House of Lords will be important to many industrial firms which keep storage or settling tanks near to water courses. If the appeal is dismissed they will not merely be under a duty to take reasonable care in using and maintaining them, but will be criminally liable for consequences they could not have foreseen. What they can be expected to foresee in each case is, of course, another matter.

Maximum penalties are fines not exceeding £50 on summary conviction, and £200 on indictment, with substantially heavier penalties including terms of imprisonment if the offence was a repetition or continuation of an earlier offence.[38] In the case of a corporation, including a nationalised industrial undertaking, the punishments can be inflicted on an officer of the corporation if he consented or connived, or if the offence was attributable to his negligence.[39] Section 3 gives the river authority preventive

35 See Impress (Worcester) v Rees [1971] 2 All E.R. 357.
36 [1971] 2 All E.R. at 913.
37 [1971] 2 All E.R. at 358.
38 R.P.P.A., 1951, s. 2(7).
39 R.P.P.A., 1951, s. 2(8).

powers by providing that where it apprehends the commission of an offence under s. 2, it may apply to a county court for an order prohibiting the discharge, or permitting it only on the terms specified in the order. The power of the court to grant an order is discretionary.

The effect of these provisions may be relaxed, however, in favour of persons wishing to discharge sewage or trade effluents into a stream. The river authority may consent to the discharge subject to such conditions as it may impose as to point of discharge, composition, temperature, volume or rate of discharge.[40] Consent shall not unreasonably be withheld, nor conditions unreasonably imposed. Appeal lies to the Ministers.[41]

Once consent has been given, the discharge does not constitute an offence under s. 2, nor under the Salmon and Freshwater Fisheries Act, 1923, s. 8,[42] nor under any bye-laws passed by a sea fishery committee.[43] Section 7 thus provides a flexible instrument by which a river authority can control the discharge of sewage and trade effluents into all inland water within its jurisdiction. The authority must from time to time review its conditions, and may after reasonable notice vary or revoke them. The Minister may direct the authority to vary or revoke conditions if he thinks fit to do so.[44]

Consent absolves a person from criminal liabilities. There is nothing in the statutes which protects him from an action at common law for damages, or a suit for injunction. Such remedies are available to any person with a legitimate interest to be protected, whether or not he has suffered damage, but of course if no damage has been suffered damages will be nominal, and the court always has a discretion to refuse to grant an injunction. Civil actions would therefore be worthwhile only in cases of actual or apprehended damage, or in order to prevent the discharge maturing into a prescriptive right to discharge.

It is also an offence to cause or knowingly permit to enter any

40 Section 7. The Clean Rivers (Estuaries and Tidal Waters) Act, 1960, extends the effect of the 1951 Act to the tidal waters and parts of the sea specified in the schedule.
41 R.P.P.A., 1961, s. 6.
42 See p. 24.
43 See p. 52.
44 R.P.P.A., 1961, s. 5.

stream any matter so as to tend, either directly or in combination with other acts of one's own or other persons, to impede the proper flow of water of the stream in a manner tending or likely to lead to a substantial aggravation of pollution. Consents may not be given by river authorities, except consent to the deposit of solid refuse on land near a stream by persons engaged in mining or quarrying.

Proceedings can be instituted only by a river authority or with the consent of the Attorney-General.[45] It is clear, therefore, that Parliament did not intend to create a right of action for breach of statutory duty.

The river authority is empowered to make bye-laws in respect of any stream or part of a stream, regulating the washing or cleansing of things in the stream, putting litter or other objectionable matter in the stream and the keeping or use on the stream of vessels provided with sanitary appliances from which polluting matter passes or can pass into the stream.[46]

Sections 2–5 of the 1951 Act, which create offences for polluting a stream and provide machinery for dealing with offenders, may be extended by Ministerial order to cover any tidal waters or parts of the sea specified in the order.[47] Of more general effect is the Clean Rivers (Estuaries and Tidal Waters) Act, 1960, which extended the powers of river authorities under the 1951 Act, s. 7, to all tidal waters and parts of the sea specified in the schedule, although it must be noted that this Act gives power only in respect of 'new discharges'.

Water Resources Act, 1963, ss. 72–5

It is an offence for any person to discharge 'by means of a well, borehole or pipe', any sewage, trade effluent or poisonous, noxious or pollutive matter into any underground stream, except with the consent of the river authority. Such consent may not unreasonably be withheld, and may be made the subject of

45 R.P.P.A., 1961, s. 11.
46 R.P.P.A., 1951, s. 5, as amended by the Act of 1961. Confirmation is by the Secretary of State for the Environment and the Minister of Agriculture, Fisheries and Food (River Boards Act, 1948, s. 18).
47 R.P.P.A., 1951. s. 6.

reasonable conditions. The authority has powers of revocation and variation; appeal lies to the Minister.

On summary conviction a fine of £100 may be imposed, and on indictment a fine with no limit specified.

The working of the section seems to place an unnecessary limitation on the powers of the river authority. Toxic wastes may be dumped or discharged into old mineshafts to poison underground water supplies with the river authority powerless to prosecute. Requests to extend this jurisdiction have not led to any success, but an alternative means of control may be applied by giving local authorities jurisdiction over all tipping within their areas.

Statutory water undertakers are also given powers to protect their sources of supply, including underground sources. This is dealt with under a separate heading on pp. 47–9.

Public Health Act, 1936, s. 259

This section provides that it is a statutory nuisance for any person to reduce any pond, pool or ditch to such a state that it is so foul as to be prejudicial to health or a nuisance.[48]

Salmon and Freshwater Fisheries Act, 1923, ss. 8 and 59

It is an offence to cause or knowingly permit to flow, or put or knowingly permit to be put, into any water containing fish, any liquid or solid matter to such an extent as to cause the water to be poisonous or injurious to fish, or the spawning grounds, spawn or food of fish. The section creates an absolute prohibition, therefore no intention is necessary, but no person can be guilty if he is ignorant that the matter is entering the stream, or could not by the exercise of reasonable care have prevented it.[49] The section also applies to tributaries to rivers containing fish.[50]

Proceedings can be taken only by the fishery authority, or by

48 For an explanation of 'Statutory nuisance' see Section 4, 'Air Pollution'.
49 Moses and Midland Railway (1915) 84 L.J.K.B. 2181. See also p. 20 *supra*.
50 See Evans v Owens [1895] 1 Q.B. 237, Moses v Iggo [1906] 1 K.B. 510.

a person certified to by the Minister of Agriculture, Fisheries and Food as having a material interest in the waters alleged to be affected.

No account is to be taken of any radioactivity possessed by any substance or article,[51] but of course the disposal of radioactive substances is strictly controlled by other statutes.[52]

Pollutants may leave fish in apparent good health, yet have the effect of tainting the flesh of the animal, thus making it commercially not worth while catching. Whether or not such tainting is 'poisonous or injurious to the fish' is doubtful, although it must be remembered that the intention of the legislature was to protect the interests of fishermen rather than the fish themselves.

Section 59(1)(p) gives a fishery authority power to make byelaws to regulate the disposal or discharge in any waters containing fish, of any liquid or solid matter specified therein detrimental to salmon, trout, freshwater fish, or the spawn or food of such fish. This power is now exercisable by any river authority with jurisdiction over that river.

Sewage trade effluents discharged into local authority sewers

Public health authorities have a duty to provide such public sewers as may be necessary for effectively draining their district for the purposes of the Public Health Act, 1936, and to make such provision, by means of sewage disposal works or otherwise, as may be necessary for effectually dealing with the contents of their sewers.[53] They also have a duty to maintain, cleanse and empty all public sewers vested in them.[54] Nevertheless they are not authorised to pollute any stream, create any nuisance, or injuriously affect any reservoir, stream, etc, so as to deprive anyone of rights in relation to such waters as are protected by law.[55]

Owner or occupiers of premises are entitled to connect their

51 Radioactive Substances Act, 1960, s. 9(1), (2)(a), and schedule 1, part 1.
52 See Section 3, 'Nuclear energy'.
53 P.H.A., 1936, s. 14.
54 P.H.A., 1936, s. 23.
55 P.H.A., 1936, ss. 30, 31 and 331, dealt with on p. 14 *supra*.

drains or sewers with the local authority sewer, and to discharge thereinto any domestic sewage and surface water.[56] This does not apply, however, to trade effluents, which are subject to special provision. Also they commit an offence if they discharge, or suffer or permit to be discharged, into any public sewer matter likely to injure the sewer, interfere with its free flow, prejudicially affect the treatment and disposal of its contents, or certain matters such as petroleum spirit specified in the section.[57]

Trade effluents are dealt with by the Public Health (Drainage of Trade Premises) Act, 1937, and the Public Health Act, 1961. 'Trade effluents' excludes domestic sewage, from whatever premises it derives, but includes effluents from agriculture and horticulture.[58]

In the case of trade effluents which had been discharged into public sewers at any time during the year ending 3 March 1937, provided that the former daily quantity and rate of discharge is not exceeded, no consent of the local authority is necessary.[59] The local authority is empowered, however, to impose charges on the occupier responsible.[60]

Any 'new discharges' of trade effluents require the consent of the local authority.[61] The authority may consent subject to conditions as to nature or composition of the effluent, maximum daily quantity and rate of discharge, elimination or diminution of any specified constituent, etc.[62] But first the authority must notify and obtain the approval of any interested body.[63] 'Interested body' is defined as any joint sewerage authority or other sewerage authority into whose sewers or sewage works the effluent is discharged, and any harbour or conservancy authority having jurisdiction over harbour or tidal waters into which the authority directly or indirectly discharges its effluent. Once imposed, the conditions may from time to time be varied,

56 P.H.A., 1936, s. 27. This is provided they have the right to take their drains or sewers across any intervening lands.
57 P.H.A., 1936, s. 27.
58 See D.T.P.A., 1937, s. 14(1), as amended by P.H.A., 1961, s. 63.
59 D.T.P.A., 1937, s. 4.
60 P.H.A., 1961, s. 55(1) and (2).
61 P.H.A., 1961, s. 1.
62 D.T.P.A., 1937, s. 2(3), and P.H.A., 1961, s. 59.
63 D.T.P.A., 1937, s. 2(4).

but not more frequently than once every two years.[64] There are special provisions relating to laundries.[65]

The local authority is also empowered to enter into an agreement with the owner or occupier of trade premises for the reception and disposal of its trade effluent. This agreement may include provision for the construction of works required for such disposal, and for repayment of the cost of those works, in whole or in part, by the owner or occupier.[66]

The local authority is therefore subject to pressure from two sides. It is bound to receive domestic sewage and all pre-1937 discharges of trade effluents. On the other hand it is bound to comply with the conditions laid down by any river authority into whose streams it discharges, and may be liable in damages and restrained by injunction if its effluents damage the interests of persons downstream.[67]

This is at first sight a perilous position, considering the growth of many urban areas and the enormous amount of sewage produced. Further difficulties arise for authorities with combined drainage systems in times of heavy rain. It must be remembered, however, that the conditions imposed by the river authorities must be reasonable and that the representatives of the constituent local authorities have a statutory majority on the board of the river authority.[68] The requirements of common law are more stringent and less flexible, and the authority cannot rely on the growth of its population as an excuse for increased pollution of rivers.[69] The courts normally grant time for new sewage works to be built, as in the Pride of Derby case, and in theory at least the authority usually has control of further development under the Town and Country Planning Act. There is also a power in the Minister, where he considers it desirable for reasons connected with the prevention of river pollution, to order a joint board to be formed to serve the sewage disposal

64 P.H.A., 1961, s. 60.
65 D.T.P.A., 1937, s. 4(4); P.H.A., 1961, s. 65.
66 D.T.P.A., 1937, s. 7(1).
67 Note P.H.A., 1936, ss. 30, 31, 331, already dealt with on p. 14, and D.T.P.A., 1937, s. 13.
68 W.R.A., 1963, s. 6(2).
69 See Pride of Derby v British Celanese and others (1953) Ch. 149. An outline of the facts and decision is given under the heading 'Common law' at p. 13 *supra*.

needs of several districts, or authorise a local authority to discharge into the sewers or disposal works of another authority.

These legal difficulties are surmountable. A more intractable
practical difficulty facing local authorities is that the increasing
problem of sewage disposal threatens to run into a head-on
collision with the growing demand for water and the need to
abstract potable waters from rivers.[70]

Their position with regard to trade effluents is easier. Where
they are bound to receive effluents they can now charge, presumably to cover the additional cost of treatment and disposal.[71]
In other cases they can withhold consent, impose conditions or
come to an agreement under the Public Health (Drainage of
Trade Premises) Act, 1937, s. 7. Difficult problems of treatment
and disposal of effluents from new processes can be dealt with
under the present system by an agreement under which additional costs are met by the producer.

River authorities

River authorities occupy the key position in the system of
statutory control. They control the use of water resources, and
they protect the waters of streams in their areas, and in some
cases the waters of estuaries and parts of the sea. In practice
these are the controls on which reliance must be placed. It is
clear that the existence of rights at common law does little to
prevent the pollution of rivers.

Control of pollution is exercised by the river authorities by
means of the conditions they attach to their consents under the
Rivers (Prevention of Pollution) Acts. These powers, backed
by the power to prosecute offenders, form a flexible instrument
so that, as far as is practicable, the degree of pollution can be
controlled after taking into account the needs of industry, the
need for sewage outlets for extra populations, and any other
relevant considerations. They will grow more important as the
demand for potable water increases. The constitution and

70 See the Jeger Report, Ministry of Housing and Local Government,
   Taken for Granted, H.M.S.O., London, 1970, para. 13, p. 3.
71 See Ministry of Housing and Local Government circular No. 46/61,
   paras. 12–14.

character of these authorities is therefore of considerable importance.

River authorities were established by the Water Resources Act, 1963. Each is a corporation with twenty-one to thirty-one members.[72] The members are appointed as follows:

Section 6(2)

Such number as is sufficient, but not more than sufficient, to form a majority to be appointed by or on behalf of all the constituent councils. These persons need not be members of the councils.[73]

Section 6(3)

To be appointed by the Minister of Agriculture, Fisheries and Food, one or more members from each of the following categories:

(a) qualified in respect of—

land drainage generally
or protection of land against erosion
or encroachment by the sea
or any other particular aspect of land drainage.

(b) qualified in respect of fisheries
(c) qualified in respect of agriculture.

Section 6(3)

To be appointed by the Secretary of State for the Environment, one or more members from each of the following categories:

(d) qualified in respect of public water supply
(e) qualified in respect of industry other than agriculture.

Section 8

Additional members

(2) The Yorkshire Ouse and Hull River Authority, and the Trent River Authority each shall include one additional member to be appointed by the National Coal Board.

72 W.R.A., 1963, s. 6(1). The Minister (now the Secretary of State for the Environment) has a discretion to increase this number. See s. 6(5).
73 W.R.A., 1963, s. 7(1).

(3) There may be provision for an additional member or members to be appointed by the Minister of Transport where

  (a) the work of the authority will have exceptionally important functions relating to navigation, or

  (b) the work of the authorities will affect to an exceptional extent the functions of a navigation authority, harbour authority or conservancy authority in relation to a navigable waterway or harbour in the area.

(4) The Minister of Agriculture, Fisheries and Food may appoint not more than two additional members, where for any year a drainage charge has been levied on the occupiers within the area. These additional members are to be chosen from persons appearing to represent those occupiers.

The river authorities thus have a statutory majority of local authority members. Those members are appointed to represent the local authorities,[74] but this does not necessarily mean that the interests of the local inhabitants are thereby indirectly represented. In the first place, not all local authority areas are represented, and where they are, the member is not answerable to the local electorate for his work on the river authority. It is doubtful if pollution of rivers has ever been a local election issue, and it is doubtful, even now, if the members have to concern themselves about the force of public opinion on this issue. It is interesting to note that representations and complaints to the river authority seem to be made more often direct to the officers rather than through local authority representatives.

The local authority members are concerned to represent rather the local authority interests, particularly as users of the rivers for discharge of sewage effluent and as those who must bear the main financial burden of pollution control. Improvements in river authority control can affect the local authorities in two ways: they can increase the demand on the rates by the river authority, and they can increase the cost of sewage treatment. Those who sit as representatives on the river authority must therefore balance the cause of purer rivers against the effect on the local rates. This effect on the rates is, of course, a legitimate public interest, but not the only one. Members of

74 See Hansard, 1962–63, vol. 676, para. 38.

the public are interested in amenity, fishing, and other recreational facilities, but these powers are hardly ever used.[75]

The interest of the public is now far wider than a mere interest in the provision of potable water and the reduction of the rate burden, and the river authority's accountability to the local public merits reconsideration.

It was noted in the introduction[76] that where standards of environmental quality are determined regionally or locally, it is appropriate for the determining authority to be responsible regionally or locally. If the members of that authority are directly responsible to the local electorate, as in the case of a borough council, no difficulties arise. The operation of this form of local accountability can best be seen in the application of the Clean Air Acts: in deciding whether or not to declare a smoke control area, councillors respond to local needs and local opinion.

Where, however, the members of the determining authority are nominated by elected bodies, as in the case of river authorities, accountability in less direct, less effective, and in some cases of no effect at all. Local authority members of a river authority do not necessarily respond to public opinion. They may vote in what they consider to be the interests of their local authorities, or in what they consider to be the interests of the general public in environmental quality. Both are proper exercises of their powers, but in the latter case they have no guidance, nor are they subject to political control. The experience of river authority officers is that they are often influenced by their background as farmers, fishermen or the like. There is not necessarily anything improper in this, and indeed a man cannot help but be influenced by his background: the significant point is the lack of political restraint. It also means that the the representation of interests on the authority is haphazard. There is therefore a case for direct election of representatives

75 There are now one or two major schemes in which river authorities will, in co-operation with nearby local authorities, develop areas of high amenity value with recreation facilities, e.g. Strathclyde park scheme. See also the *Dee Crossing Study, Phase 1, A report to the technical working party*, H.M.S.O., London, 1967.

76 See p. 5 *supra*.

to these authorities, or for the constitution to provide for the representation of the affected local interests.[77]

These considerations may grow in importance if recommendations made in two recent reports are put into effect. The Jeger report recommended that the jurisdiction of river authorities should be extended to sea areas as far as the three-mile limit,[78] and supported the suggestion that they should control the whole of the water cycle, including sewage disposal. The Central Advisory Water Committee report[79] outlined four alternative systems of control over the water cycle, each recommending the establishment of a regional water authority. In each case the recommendation is for an authority with a very wide area of jurisdiction and extensive powers. One has only to combine the recommendations of the two reports to see what enormous jurisdictions would be created. These will be powerful authorities controlling the quality of a significant, and to many people important, part of our environment. If the democratic principles which as a nation we accept are to be logically applied, those authorities are to be accountable to the public they serve. To the extent that they serve a local public and local interests, that public and those interests are entitled to proper and effective representation.

River authorities and effective pollution control

We have seen that river authorities have been given statutory powers to prevent or limit pollution of rivers within the areas of their jurisdictions. Once houses and factories have been built, however, the use of these powers is, in practice, limited. Occupiers of domestic premises have a statutory right to discharge into local authority sewers, and although in theory the

---

77 It was implied in the second reading of the water resources Bill that appointed members were to be regarded as representing interests. The wording of the Act suggests that they are there to contribute from their experience and expertise. See Hansard, 1962–63, vol. 676, para. 50. Note also that they appear in river authority annual reports as representing interests.
78 *Taken for Granted*, para. 268.
79 Central Advisory Water Committee, *The Future Management of Water in England and Wales*, H.M.S.O. for the Department of the Environment, London, 1971.

river authority can control the discharge into its rivers, in practice it is not possible to compel a local authority to comply immediately with its requirements. The same is true to a lesser degree of factory premises. River authority officials would quite rightly hesitate to impose restrictions which would stop or curtail the factory's production. In order to carry out its duties effectively, therefore, the river authority must have prior notice of any intended development which might affect the quality of its waters.

In general, local authorities are very co-operative in this matter, but practice is not uniform. Local planning authorities normally inform the river authority of planning applications which might affect them, and take note of their representations. It is sometimes possible to indicate to the firm proposing to build a factory what kind of discharge will be acceptable. Many river authorities would like to see a statutory obligation placed on the local planning authority to inform them of certain classes of planning applications. The latter vigorously oppose this proposal, and there seems little prospect of its being accepted, but an administrative direction to the same effect would probably serve the purpose almost as well, without giving rise to any legal difficulties.

The most frequent complaint under this head is that local authorities do not inform river authorities when they accept an industrial discharge into their sewers. Ingredients of the discharge such as salts of heavy metals may pass through the sewage works without causing trouble, and into watercourses, where they may be toxic to aquatic life. The local authority must inform and obtain the approval of any 'interested body', but unfortunately this term is not defined so as to include river authorities.[80]

Even when there is a breach of existing conditions, river authorities are not quick to prosecute.[81] The offender may be a firm or local authority finding difficulty in complying with conditions. In some cases the discharge is 'accidental', but such accidents are often the result of bad maintenance. The maxi-

80 See p. 26 *supra*.
81 In 1968 there were only thirty-three prosecutions in England and Wales, leading to fines in twenty-three cases.

mum penalty is £100, and even this is rarely imposed. There is a case for increasing the maximum substantially so that firms can be persuaded to improve their standards of care and maintenance.

River authorities are even more reluctant to use the procedure provided by Rivers (Prevention of Pollution) Act, 1951, s. 3, under which an application may be made to a county court for an order compelling a person to comply with the conditions of the consent to discharge into the river. The reluctance is difficult to understand. This is a flexible instrument, for the court can attach conditions to its order.

The river authority is thus the guardian of the general public's interest in clean rivers. The case for making it responsible to the local public is strengthened by the fact that no machinery is provided by which the public or interested parties can directly influence to grant consent to a proposed discharge. This position is the result of Rivers (Prevention of Pollution) Act, 1961, s. 12, which provides:

(1) If any person discloses any information—

> (a) which has been furnished to or obtained by him in connection with an application for consent, or the imposition of conditions, under this Act or the principal Act (including variation of conditions, and references and applications to the Minister); or
> (b) which is derived from a sample of effluent taken for the purposes of this Act or the principal Act,

he shall be guilty of an offence, unless the disclosure is made

> (i) with the consent of the person by whom the information was furnished or from whom it was obtained or, in the case of information derived from a sample of effluent, of the person making the discharge in question; or
> (ii) in connection with the execution of this Act or the principal Act; or
> (iii) for the purposes of any proceedings arising out of this Act or the principal Act (including references and applications to the Minister) or of any criminal proceedings whether so arising or not, or for the purpose of any report of such proceedings.

This section did not appear in the 1951 Act, nor as a clause in the 1961 Bill as originally drafted: it was inserted on representations made on behalf of industry after the Bill had had its second reading in the House of Commons. Industry's claim is that this is a necessary protection against competitors. This may undoubtedly be true of a firm carrying out research and development work, or using catalysts in the course of its ordinary production. In most cases the dangers of disclosure will be considerably less, and are to be balanced against the protection of other interests, both private and public.

The result of the present provision is that there can be no rights of objection or even rights to make representations. Rights of appeal to the Secretary of State are limited to disappointed applicants: no riparian owners or other persons affected by a consent to discharge, not even a sea fisheries committee, can appeal against the consent. The man who wishes to run a new discharge into a river certainly has to satisfy the river authority, but he is not exposed to cross-examination by the legal representatives of a person who might be seriously affected by the effluent.

Industry reveals facts about its discharges when a public enquiry is held, with little protest or complaint. There is a case for replacing the blanket protection given by s. 12 with a right to apply for non-disclosure, the onus lying on the firm concerned to establish the justification for secrecy.

At present, those with legal interests to protect, such as riparian owners and holders of fishing rights, can protect their interests by an action at common law. Others who suffer over and above the general public may also have a right of action for public nuisance.[82] But in practice they must all wait until they have received the polluting effluent and identify its source before they can bring an action.

The general public, on the other hand, must rely on public authorities acting on their behalf. Amongst this 'general public' there are many people who have an 'interest' in rivers, not being an interest in the legal sense and having no connection with property rights, but none the less genuine, in some cases substantial, and certainly worthy of protection. In 1851 Parke B. said,[83] 'Flowing water is publici juris ... It is public and

82 See p. 55 *supra*.
83 Embery *v* Owen (1851) 155 E.R. 579. For a fuller quotation see
   p. 12 *supra*.

common in the sense that all who have a right of access to it
may reasonably use it.' Unfortunately, 'all who have a right of
access' are in English law a limited class of people. There are
now many who have the opportunity to use rivers for recreational purposes although they have no legal right of access, and
now that visual amenity is accepted as important, the range of
'interested people' is wide indeed. It would seem proper to give
them a right of objection to proposed polluting discharges.

Those with common law rights have an even stronger case.
It must be remembered that their right is to water 'undiminished
in quantity or quality'[84] and that any degree of pollution gives
them a right of action. There seems no reason why these people
should not be given rights to object, and the same rights of
appeal as applicants to discharge now have. Their rights would
in no way be diminished, and they would have the advantage of
an inexpensive remedy in the first place.

Statutory water undertakers

No account of the protection of inland waters from pollution
can ignore the position of statutory water undertakers. They
have a duty to maintain a supply of potable water, and powers
to protect their sources of supply. They also control a significant part of the water cycle.

The growing demand for potable water makes the protection
of inland waters a more urgent problem. The need to abstract
from rivers will increase, and already some of our rivers con-
sist substantially of effluent from sewage works. In the words of
the Jeger committee, 'We cannot keep some of our rivers flowing in dry weather without returned sewage effluent.'[85] It has
been estimated that the volume of sewage will double by the
end of the century, and that the demand for water will also
double.[86] The combination of these two trends means that
alternative sources of supply must be found, or that the quality
of river water must be considerably improved. The solution may
lie in a combination of both, but in so far as the demand on

84 See p. 12 *supra*.
85 *Taken for Granted*, para. 14, p. 3.
86 *Ibid*. para. 13, p. 3.

rivers will increase, pollution by local authorities and industry must be reduced. It is unlikely that, as both population and the standard of living continue to rise, the volume of sewage will decrease. It follows that far higher standards of treatment, either by the local authorities or by the statutory undertakers, will become necessary.

The problem of water supply is thus inseparable from pollution control. This has led to the suggestion, made from a number of quarters in recent years, that the whole of the water cycle should be placed under the control of a single authority.[87] This is too large and complex a subject for discussion here. For our purposes it will suffice to explain the present position of statutory water undertakers so far as is relevant to the problem of environmental control.

A 'statutory water undertaker' is defined as 'any company, local authority, board, committee, or other person authorised by a local enactment to supply water and any local authority or board supplying water under the Public Health Act, 1936'.[88] In 1970, of the statutory water undertakings in England and Wales sixty-four were local authorities, 101 joint boards and thirty-three statutory companies. There were also a few private systems of water supply, usually in rural areas and each serving fewer than a hundred people.[89] Most undertakers treat all their water to standards suitable for drinking, but some supply industrial water of a lower standard.

Water companies

The older companies were incorporated by private Act of Parliament. These private Acts usually adopted the Waterworks Clauses Acts, 1847 and 1863, relating to the supply of water, the Companies Clauses Acts, 1845–89, by which the conduct of the companies' affairs was strictly controlled, and the Lands Clauses Acts, 1845–83, dealing with powers to

87 The most recent and authoritative recommendations are those of the Central Advisory Water Committee, *op. cit.*
88 W.A., 1948, s. 1.
89 See *The Future Management of Water in England and Wales.*

acquire land. Although many of these Acts have been repealed
wholly or in part, their provisions remain in force for the statutory water undertakers which adopted them. The private Acts
of Parliament by which the companies were established normally
granted powers to make bye-laws, and many of these provisions
also remain in force today.

The Gas and Water Facilities Acts, 1870 and 1873, provided
a simpler method for establishing water companies. They could
be established as water undertakers by a provisional order,
subsequently confirmed by Parliament, and incorporated under
the current Companies Act. The provisional order would adopt
the provisions of the Water Clauses Act and the Land Clauses
Acts. Under the Gas and Water Facilities Acts existing companies could also acquire further powers.

The use of the various Clauses Acts meant that the companies were governed by a substantially uniform code. Even the
provisions of the many private Acts would be fairly similar,
and some may well have been modified by the Minister to bring
them into line with general legislation.[90]

Finally, some of the provisions of the Water Acts, 1945–58,
apply to the companies.

The conduct of the companies' affairs remains strictly controlled. For example, the issue of shares and stock and the
distribution of dividends are governed by statutory provisions,
and by the Water Act, 1945, s. 42. Abstracts of the accounts
of the company, in such form as the Minister may direct, are to
be sent annually to the Minister and all local authorities within
whose districts they supply water or have waterworks.

Local authorities and joint water boards

Many local authorities which are also statutory water under-
takers derive powers from private Acts of Parliament. The older
Acts will have incorporated the clauses of Waterworks Clauses
Acts, 1847 and 1863. Other local authorities and joint water

90 The Minister is given power to repeal or amend a local enactment
   on the application of a statutory water undertaker by W.A., 1945,
   s. 33.

boards are governed by Public Health Act, 1936, and Water Acts, 1945–58. Their powers and duties are to be found principally in the Water Act, 1945, third schedule, which provides a fairly comprehensive code. As a result of these provisions it appears that there are local authorities which are governed to some extent both by the old code and by the new. They may also have additional powers granted by subsequent private Acts.

All councils of boroughs, urban districts and rural districts are under a duty to see that there is a sufficient supply of wholesome water in their areas.[91] For districts in which there are schools or houses they must provide a piped supply of wholesome water, except where it is not practicable to do this at reasonable cost.[92]

For the purpose of providing their districts with a supply of water, local authorities and joint water boards are empowered to construct, take on lease, or with the approval of the Minister purchase, a waterworks.[93] They may also contract with any other local authority or persons for a supply of water.[94] There are, however, certain restrictions on these powers to prevent them from taking over the functions of an existing statutory water undertaker in the area.[95]

Many local authorities have additional powers both to abstract and supply water granted by private Acts of Parliament in more recent years.

Creation of statutory water undertakers and grant of further powers by Ministerial order

The Water Act, 1945, s. 23, empowers the Minister to make orders granting certain powers to persons who are or propose to become statutory water undertakers. This is now the simplest method by which an existing person can be given the status of statutory water undertaker.

91 P.H.A., 1936, s. 111, as amended by W.A., 1945, s. 28.
92 P.H.A., 1936, s. 116; W.A., 1945, s. 28.
93 P.H.A., 1936, s. 116.
94 P.H.A., 1936, s. 116(1) (IV).
95 P.H.A., 1936, ss. 116 and 117.

Combination of statutory water undertakers

The Minister is empowered, on application or by compulsion, to provide for:[96]

- (a) supply of water jointly by two or more statutory water undertakers;
- (b) joint boards or joint committees;
- (c) amalgamation of statutory water undertakers who are not local authorities;
- (d) transfer of part or the whole of a water undertaking.

Limits of supply

In granting statutory powers to water undertakers Parliament or the Minister, as the case may be, defines the area in which supplies of water may be provided.

Licences to abstract water

The Water Resources Act, 1963, puts water resources under the control of river authorities. No person is permitted to abstract water from a source without a licence granted by the local authority for that area.[97] There are exceptions to this requirement[98] and the Minister is empowered to make further exceptions.[99]

Statutory water undertakers are governed by these provisions in the same way as other persons, but in many cases they will have been entitled to licences as of right. The Water Resources Act, 1963, s. 33, provides:

A person is entitled to a licence as of right if

- (a) he was entitled to abstract water from a source of supply under any statutory provision in force on the second appointed day.

or

- (b) he had extracted water from a source of supply otherwise

96 W.A., 1945, s. 9.
97 W.R.A., 1963, s. 23.
98 W.R.A., 1963, s. 24.
99 W.R.A., 1963, s. 25.

than under a statutory provision during the period of five years ending with the second appointed day.[100]

The provisions of a licence granted as of right, including those relating to quantity of water to be extracted, shall be such as appear to the river authority to correspond as near as may be to the statutory provision under which he was entitled to abstract, or if no quantity was specified therein, the quantity he had extracted during the five-year period.[101]

The Minister is authorised to control abstractions during periods of drought[102] and, of course, modern private Acts of Parliament may confer rights to abstract.

Finance

Charges for domestic supply are by a rate poundage on the net annual value of the premises; other forms of charge may be made by agreement.[103] Certain additional powers have been acquired by private Act of Parliament by some statutory water undertakers[104] and the Minister is in certain circumstances empowered to vary charges.[105]

Duties of statutory water undertakers to supply water

Companies governed by the Water Clauses Acts, 1847 and 1863

Assuming a company adopted without variation all the provisions of the Waterworks Clauses Acts, 1847 and 1863, it would be under an obligation to provide water for domestic purposes.[106]

The company would have a duty to cause pipes to be laid down and water to be brought to every part of the town or district within

100 But see W.R.A., 1963, s. 33(3).
101 W.R.A., 1963, s. 34.
102 W.A., 1958, s. 1.
103 See W.C.A., 1847, s. 68; P.H.A., 1936, ss. 126–8; W.A., 1948, s. 12; W.A., 1945, schedule 3, s. 46.
104 See C. A. Cross, *Principles of Local Government Law*, third edition, Sweet & Maxwell, London, 1966, p. 425.
105 W.A., 1945, s. 40.
106 See W.W.C.A., 1863, s. 12, for the limits of 'domestic purposes'.

the limits of its supply as required by owners or occupiers of houses in that part, provided the annual aggregate water rate payable by them was not less than one-tenth of the expense of laying the pipe, and they severally bound themselves by agreement to take such supply for at least three successive years.[107] The owners or occupiers of dwelling houses within the limits of supply would have a right to lay communication pipes, subject to the owners whose land the pipes would have to cross, connect them to the company's pipes, and demand a sufficient supply of water for domestic purposes.[108]

It would then be the duty of the company to keep in the pipes laid down by them a supply of pure and wholesome water sufficient for the domestic use of all inhabitants who were entitled to demand a supply. The supply would have to be constantly laid on at sufficient pressure to make the water reach the top storey of the highest house within the limits.[107]

The Act laid down penalties for breach of this duty to supply water, subject to exceptions in times of frost, unusual drought or for unavoidable cause or accident.[109] If this section of the Act applies, the company may also be liable for breach of statutory duty to any owner or occupier entitled to a supply, and in negligence to others. In Read v Croydon Corporation[110] an occupier's daughter contracted typhoid from the corporation's drinking water. It was held that the corporation owed a duty to the occupier to exercise a high standard of skill and care to maintain the standard required by the statute, since the duty to provide water for domestic purposes was for his benefit. The statutory water undertaker was therefore liable for the special damages the occupier suffered as a result of the illness of his daughter. It was also held that the company owed a duty of care at common law to the daughter, and that therefore she was entitled to compensation for pain and suffering. It is therefore clear that the statutory duty is owed only to those who are entitled to demand a supply of water, and that it is not an absolute duty, but that a common law duty of care is owed

107 W.W.C.A., 1847, s. 35.
108 W.W.C.A., 1847, ss. 48–53.
109 W.W.C.A., 1847, s. 36.
110 [1938] 4 All E.R. 631.

to all those who might foreseeably suffer through negligent operation by the water undertaker. Since the Act requires that the company should provide and keep a supply of pure and wholesome water 'in the pipes laid down by them', contamination by lead pipes laid down by the consumer does not render them liable for breach of statutory duty.[111] But they may still be liable at common law if, through their own lack of care, foreseeable injury was suffered as a result of contamination in service pipes laid down by the consumer. In Barnes v Irwell Valley Water Board[112] the water was contaminated by lead pipes laid down by the consumer but inspected by the statutory water undertaker. The company was held to have been negligent in not either taking steps to reduce the plumbo-solvency of the water, or warning the consumers.

The word 'pure' cannot, of course, be construed literally. The Judicial Committee of the Privy Council has recently held that the addition of fluoride added no impurity to already pure water.[113] It is noteworthy that modern statutes refer simply to 'wholesome' water.

Waterworks Clauses Act, 1847, dealt also with the supply of water for public purposes. A statutory water undertaker governed by the sections was required to fix proper fire plugs to mains and other pipes and keep such pipes charged with water.[114] It was also required to provide in those pipes a sufficient supply of water for cleansing sewers and drains, cleansing and watering streets and for other public purposes.[115]

The company's duty to supply water for other non-domestic purposes is dealt with under the heading 'Duties of all statutory water undertakers' on p. 46.

The Minister may, on the application of any statutory water undertaker, by order repeal or amend any local enactment relating to the supply of water by them.[116] In certain circumstances he may also, by order, apply to any statutory water undertaker

111 Nulnes v Mayor of Huddersfield (1886) 11 A.C. 511.
112 [1938] 2 All E.R. 650.
113 Attorney-General of New Zealand v Lower Hutt Corporation (1964) A.C. 1469.
114 W.W.C.A., 1847, s. 38.
115 W.W.C.A., 1847, s. 42.
116 W.A., 1945, s. 33.

such provisions of the Water Act, 1945, third schedule, as appear to him to be appropriate.[117]

Local authorities and statutory water undertakers governed by the Water Act, 1945, third schedule

The Water Act, 1945, third schedule now provides a more modern code of laws for statutory water undertakers, but again Parliament has adhered to the practice of providing sections which can be applied or adopted. By s. 31 and the fourth schedule, certain sections of the code apply to local authorities supplying water under the Public Health Act, 1936. Other sections of the code may in certain circumstances be applied by Ministerial order to statutory water undertakers.[118] Finally, sections of the code may be adopted as were sections of the Waterworks Clauses Acts.

Local authorities supplying water may therefore be governed by local Acts of Parliament, some by several such Acts, the older ones incorporating the Waterworks Clauses Acts and the more recent giving them additional powers; they may also be governed to some extent by the new code. For practical purposes, the position of each authority requires separate and careful examination.

The schedule empowers the statutory water undertaker to lay mains within the limits of its supply and service pipes[119] under streets, and provides that the owner or occupier of premises requiring water for domestic purpose shall lay the supply pipe[119] at his own expense.[120] The statutory water undertaker must lay mains to bring water to any part of its area of supply if required to do so by owners or occupiers of premises within that area whose aggregate annual rate is not less than one-eighth of the

---

117 W.A., 1945, s. 32. But note the limitations placed on this power by s. 62, particularly the one relating to public rights of way, recreation, etc.
118 W.A., 1945, s. 32.
119 For definitions of 'service pipe', 'supply pipe' and 'communications pipe', see W.A., 1945, third schedule, s. 1, and W.A., 1948, s. 10.
120 W.A., 1945, third schedule, ss. 19, 21, 40, 41. Note the provisions relating to supply pipes under the highway.

cost of providing and laying the mains and who severally agree to take the water for at least three years.[121]

An owner or occupier within the limits of supply who has complied with requirements as to the laying of a supply pipe is entitled to demand and receive a supply of water sufficient for domestic purposes.[122] The statutory water undertaker is to provide in its mains and communication pipes a supply of wholesome water sufficient for domestic purposes.

Section 37 of the Water Act, 1945—a section in the main part of the Act which automatically applies to all statutory water undertakers—requires them to lay mains for providing new houses with water for domestic purposes on demand made by the owner of the land, but provides that he shall make a contribution towards the cost.[123]

There are provisions in the schedule requiring the statutory water undertaker at the request of the fire authority to fix fire hydrants to its mains, and in some circumstances at the request and expense of the owner or occupier of a factory or business premises.[124] Anyone may take water for extinguishing fires without charge,[125] and every main to which a fire hydrant is attached must provide a supply of water for cleansing sewers and drains, cleansing and watering streets and other public purposes.[126] There are penalties for failing to comply with these obligations, subject to exceptions in time of frost, drought or for unavoidable cause or accident or necessary works.[127]

The statutory water undertaker is to cause water in all pipes giving domestic supplies or on which hydrants are fixed to be laid on constantly and at such pressure as will cause the water to reach the top of the topmost storey of every building within the limits of supply, provided that nothing in the section shall require it to deliver water at a greater height than that to which it will flow by gravitation through mains from a service reservoir or tank, and the statutory water undertaking may at

121 W.A., 1945, third schedule, s. 29.
122 W.A., 1945, third schedule, s. 30. Note the exceptions in the proviso.
123 See W.A., 1945, s. 37; W.A., 1948, s. 14; Housing Act, 1949, s. 51.
124 W.A., 1945, third schedule, ss. 32, 35.
125 W.A., 1945, third schedule, s. 36.
126 W.A., 1945, third schedule, s. 37.
127 W.A., 1945, third schedule, s. 38.

its discretion determine from which reservoir or tank the supply is to be taken.[128] There are penalties for failure to comply, subject to the usual exceptions, which are provided for expressly without prejudice to civil liability.

Duties of all statutory water undertakers

Statutory water undertakers supplying water otherwise than in bulk shall give a supply of water on reasonable terms and conditions for non-domestic purposes to any owner or occupier of premises within the limits of supply who requests it. They are not required, however, to give such a supply if it would endanger their ability to meet existing obligations to supply water for any purposes, or probable future requirements to supply water for domestic purposes, without having to incur unreasonable expense in constructing new waterworks.[129]

Supply of water in bulk

An agreement may be made by any statutory water undertaker and any other person to supply water in bulk to any person, whether a statutory water undertaker or not. The approval of the Minister is required.[130] If the Minister considers it expedient, he may order any statutory water undertaker to supply another statutory water undertaker with water in bulk.[130]

Standards of management

The Ministry of Housing and Local Government published in 1967 'Standards to be adopted in operation and management of waterworks'. If any statutory water undertaker fails to maintain those standards, and damage results, it could be found liable in negligence.

Prevention of pollution of water supplies at common law

Statutory water undertakers may have redress by damages and injunction against anyone polluting their supply of water.

128 W.A., 1945, third schedule, s. 39.
129 W.A., 1945, s. 27.
130 W.A., 1945, s. 12, and W.A., 1948, s. 4.

Planning control

The danger of pollution is a relevant consideration in considering applications for planning consents. This applies not only to factories and other premises from which there may be discharges to watercourses, but to many kinds of development in areas where water supply is obtained from underground sources. For example, in the area of the Metropolitan Water Board there are thirty-five wells in operation: consequently there have been many public enquiries into proposals for septic tanks, cesspools, refuse disposal at caravan sites, and the like.

Prevention of pollution of water supplies under statutory provisions

The many private Acts of Parliament on water supply may, of course, include provisions for the prevention of pollution.

The Waterworks Clauses Act, 1847, s. 61, protects streams, reservoirs, aqueducts or other waterworks belonging to statutory water undertakers. It is an offence for anyone to bathe; to wash, throw or cause to enter therein any dog or other animal; to throw in any rubbish, dirt or other noisome thing; to wash or cleanse therein any cloth, wool, leather, skin of any animal, clothes or other thing; to cause water from any sink, sewer or drain or other filthy water belonging to him or under his control to run or be brought into them. This is followed by a general provision which makes it an offence to do any other act by which the water of the statutory water undertaker is fouled. In practice, many statutory water undertakers permit recreational use to be made of their reservoirs.[131]

The Water Act, 1945, s. 21, a section of general application, states that a person is guilty of an offence if, through any act of neglect of his, there is polluted or likely to be polluted any spring, well or adit from which water is used or likely to be used for human consumption, domestic purposes, or for manufacturing food or drink for human consumption. It is expressly provided, however, that the section is not to be construed as

---

131 See the British Waterworks Association, *Amenity Use of Reservoirs* survey, 'Analyses of returns', 1969.

prohibiting or restricting any method of cultivation of land which is in accordance with the principles of good husbandry, or the reasonable use of oil or tar on any highway maintainable at public expense, so long as the highway authority took reasonable steps to prevent the pollution.

Proceedings for an offence under this section, or any other provisions of the Act, if taken by any person other than the Minister, a local authority, statutory water undertaker, person aggrieved or river authority in the case of a watercourse, require the written consent of the Attorney-General.[132] It will be the duty of the local authority to prosecute if such step is necessary for the provision of a supply of wholesome water to any part of its district in which there are houses or schools.[133]

A statutory water undertaker is empowered to acquire land for the purpose of protecting against pollution any surface or underground water belonging to it, or which it is authorised to take.[134] It may also enter into an agreement with the owner or occupier of any land for the execution of works necessary, *inter alia*, for preserving the purity of water it is authorised to take.[135]

Bye-laws

Many private Acts of Parliament confer on statutory water undertakers the power to make bye-laws. Two sections of the Water Act, 1945, empower statutory water undertakers generally to make bye-laws. Under s. 17 they may make bye-laws for preventing, *inter alia*, the contamination of water supplied by them. Under s. 18 the statutory water undertaker, for the purpose of protecting against pollution any surface or underground water belonging to it or which it is authorised to take, may define the area within which it deems it necessary to exercise control and prohibit or regulate the doing within that area of any act specified in the bye-law.[136] It may also require the owner or occupier of premises within that area to execute and keep in good repair any works it considers necessary for preventing

132 W.A., 1945, s. 46.
133 W.A., 1945, s. 28, the section substituted for P.H.A., 1936, s. 111.
134 W.A., 1945, s. 22.
135 W.A., 1945, s. 15.
136 Note that this section is of wider application than s. 21 *supra*.

pollution of its water. There are, of course, rights to compensation for expenses incurred and for curtailment or injurious affection of the owner's or occupier's legal rights.

The statutory water undertaker has a duty to enforce its bye-laws, but has a power to relax their requirements or dispense with compliance in particular cases.[137]

The Minister is given power to require any statutory water undertaker to make bye-laws under ss. 17 and 18, and he may require them to revoke bye-laws and make new ones if he considers the existing ones to be unsatisfactory.

He has published a set of model bye-laws,[138] but this does not include any which may be made under ss. 17 or 18. The power in s. 18 has been used, particularly by authorities drawing water from underground sources. Extensive areas have been defined.[139] In 1969 a North Lindsey bye-law received Ministerial approval which defined an area, being that of a chalk outcrop, some 10 miles by 5½ miles approximately at its greatest dimensions.

137 W.A., 1945, s. 19.
138 1966 edition.
139 Margate, 1902: 15,000 yards from any well or adit. Brighton, 1924: radius of two miles from any well or adit.

3 Sea fisheries

Common law

The soil of the sea as far as the territorial limits is vested in the Crown. The Crown can grant rights in this soil, e.g. the right to extract minerals, but such rights are granted subject to the public rights of navigation and fishing.[1] An individual can also acquire title to this soil by usage and prescription.[2]

Prima facie the Crown has title to all the foreshore and to the soil of all navigable rivers as far as the tide flows and reflows,[1] therefore there are no private riparian rights. The Crown can, however, grant rights to other persons and persons can acquire rights by adverse possession. Likewise easements such as rights of way may be acquired over the foreshore and rights acquired by legal custom.[3] Subject to such rights, therefore, the public has no right of passage over the foreshore,[4] not even the right to cross to get to or from boats.[5] Nor has the public any right to bathe from the foreshore.[6]

The Crown could grant a several right to fish, but was restrained by Magna Carta from granting exclusive rights of fishery in the sea or tidal waters; therefore there can now be no presumption of any subsequent grant from long usage. In these waters the public retains a right to fish and a right to navigate, with all rights incidental thereto, and no grants by the Crown can derogate from these rights. Lord Westbury L.C. put this in plain terms when he said:[7]

1 Gann *v* Free Fisheries of Whitstable (1865) 11 E.R. 1305.
2 Gann *v* Free Fisheries of Whitstable (1865) 11 E.R. 1305 and Foreman *v* Whitstable Free Fisheries (1869) L.R. 6 H.L.
3 Mercer *v* Dunne [1905] 2 Ch.
4 Maddock *v* Wallasey Local Board (1886) 55 L.J.Q.B. 267.
5 Blundell *v* Catterall (1821) 106 E.R. 129; but see Brickman *v* Walters [1904] 2 Ch. 313; Behrens *v* Richards [1905] 2 Ch. 614.
6 See Beckett *v* Lyons [1967] 1 All E.R. 833 at 842 and 854.
7 Goodman *v* Mayor of Saltash (1882) 7 App. Cas. 633.

The bed of all navigable rivers where the tide flows and reflows, and of all estuaries or arms of the sea, is by law vested in the Crown. But this ownership of the Crown is for the benefit of the subject, and cannot be used in a manner so as to derogate from, or interfere with, the right of navigation, which belongs by law to the subjects of the realm. The right to anchor is a necessary part of the right of navigation, because it is essential for the full enjoyment of that right. If the Crown therefore grants part of the bed or soil of an estuary or navigable river, the grantee takes subject to the public right, and he cannot in respect of his ownership of the soil make any claim or demand, even if it is expressly granted to him, which in any way interferes with the enjoyment of the public right.

This applies equally to the right to fish, but such public right is coextensive only with tidal waters. The right to navigate may go beyond.

Thus persons may have acquired private rights which the law still protects. Where, for example, a person has been granted a right to the soil of the foreshore, he may bring an action in nuisance against any person who so pollutes the sea as adversely to affect his occupation of that land.[8] In Foster v Warblington U.D.C.[9] the plaintiff did not own any of the sea shore, but had sufficient occupation of part of it where he had 'oyster ponds' for fattening oysters to give him a right of action against the urban district council, which contaminated the oysters by sewage effluent. Where pollution has affected public rights, such as the right to fish in tidal waters, an action can be brought only with the sanction and in the name of the Attorney-General, unless the plaintiff can show that he has suffered direct damage over and above that suffered by the public at large, in which case he can bring an action in his own name.

Even the Crown has no right to use the foreshore or other land so as to create a nuisance; therefore the Crown cannot grant rights to use land so as to create a nuisance.

8   See Esso Petroleum v Southport Corporation [1956] A.C. 218.
9   [1906] 1 K.B. 648.

Statutory control

Sea Fisheries Regulation Act, 1966

The establishment of sea fisheries districts and local fisheries
committees is provided for by the Sea Fisheries Regulation Act,
1966. By s. 1 the Minister of Agriculture, Fisheries and Food,
on the application of a county council or borough council, may
create a district comprising any part of the sea within national
territorial waters adjacent to England or Wales either with or
without any part of the adjoining coast. He may also provide
for the constitution of a local fisheries committee. The Minister
has in fact created eleven such fisheries comprising the whole
of the coastline, with the exception of a short strip of coastline
opposite the Ministry of Agriculture, Fisheries and Food laboratory at Lowestoft.

Where a sea fisheries district adjoins or overlaps the area of
a river authority, the Minister is required to draw a dividing
line at or near the mouth of every river or estuary so as to
define the limits of the sea fishery.[10]

The order creating the committee must provide that it shall
be a committee of a county council or borough council, or a
joint committee of such councils.[11] Members must be

(*a*) appointed by the council or constituent councils
(*b*) additional members, not exceeding in number the council
appointees, as follows
   (i) one person appointed by each river authority having
jurisdiction within the district of the committee.
   (ii) the rest appointed by the Minister as being acquainted
with the needs and opinions of fishing interests in that
district.

A local sea fisheries committee is empowered to make bye-
laws for the purpose, *inter alia*, of prohibiting or regulating the
deposit or discharge of any solid or liquid substance detrimental
to sea fish or sea fishing.[12] The bye-laws require confirmation by
the Minister, who also has power to revoke them.[13] The Act,
however, subordinates these bye-laws to the power of the river

10 S.F.R.A., 1966, s. 18(1).
11 S.F.R.A., 1966, s. 2
12 S.F.R.A., 1966, s. 5(1)(*c*).
13 S.F.R.A., 1966, s. 7(1).

authorities to grant consents to discharges, and to statutory powers of local authorities to discharge sewage effluent.[14]

There is no authority specially charged with the duty of preventing or controlling pollution of the coastline and coastal sea. Sea fisheries committees were established, of course, solely to protect fishing interests, but not all of them interpret their powers in the same way. Some interpret them narrowly, being prepared to act only when there is evidence of damage to fish or fishing interests. Others consider that any pollution which affects the ecology of the area must necessarily affect their interests, and therefore to some extent adopt the role of pollution control authorities.

Sea fisheries committee bye-laws vary. Some merely prohibit the deposit or discharge of substances detrimental to sea or sea fishing;[15] others impose a similar prohibition, but provide that the committee may grant consents to which conditions may be attached. A bye-law submitted to the Minister for confirmation by Lancashire and Western Sea Fisheries Joint Committee not only gives the power to grant consents subject to conditions but also gives 'detrimental to sea or sea fishing' a wide meaning, grants power to vary conditions, and provides for an appeal to the Minister. This will give the committee powers similar to those of a river authority within the limits of its jurisdiction.

It is these limits on the jurisdiction of the committees that render full control over pollution of the coastal sea area impossible. Local authorities with statutory powers, specific or general, to discharge sewage into the sea may do so by pipeline and the local sea fisheries committee is powerless to control the discharges. Moreover, these authorities may have accepted industrial waste into their sewers. Local authorities must first gain the approval of 'interested bodies' before accepting trade effluents into their sewers. It is odd that the term 'interested bodies' is still limited to other sewerage authorities which might be affected, harbour and conservancy authorities which have jurisdictions in harbours and tidal waters, and does not include sea fisheries committees.[16]

14 S.F.R.A., 1966. s. 6(*b*) and (*c*) and see p. 22 *supra*.
15 North Eastern, Northumberland and Eastern.
16 D.T.P.A., 1937, ss. 2(4) and 14(1); P.H.A., 1961, s. 55(4); Merchant Shipping Act, 1894, s. 742.

Neither have the committees any control over, nor even a formal right of objection to, what is discharged into rivers. River authorities do send prior notice of the consents they are about to give and are prepared to take note of fisheries committee objections. In some cases they are even prepared to monitor for substances the committee considers noxious. Attitudes vary, however. If the rivers contain fish, the interests of the two authorities are broadly similar: if they do not, there may be a clash of interests, with the sea fisheries committee in the weaker position.

The sea fisheries committees thus have a limited jurisdiction over a narrow strip of coastal water, and lie sandwiched between sources of pollution over which they have no control. On the one side rivers and local authority outfalls bring effluents, admittedly enormously diluted by the sea but sometimes containing metal salts which may be toxic. On the other side, there is pollution coming from beyond the territorial limit. Of course, there are the Oil in Navigable Waters Acts and the Ministry of Agriculture scheme of supervision over sea dumping,[17] but in both cases it is doubtful if there is sufficient surveillance to ensure protection.

The Jeger committee recommended that the jurisdiction of river authorities should be extended to sea areas as far as the three-mile limit.[18] Recent trends in the disposal of wastes, however, have led to suggestions both in this country and abroad that there is a need for the control of sea disposals beyond territorial waters. According to the Geneva Convention on the Continental Shelf, 1958, a State may exploit the living resources of the sea bed on its continental shelf.[18] It would be surprising if adequate steps necessary to protect those resources were not taken.[19]

Given the present situation, it would seem more logical to give the sea fisheries committees' powers to a more powerful body controlling pollution of a sea area going beyond the present limit of three miles. The constitution of such a body or bodies and the area of its jurisdiction raise questions too complex for discussion here.

17 See p. 109 *infra*.
18 *Taken for Granted*, para. 268.
19 Cf. Continental Shelf Act, 1964; see p. 97 *infra*.

4   Air pollution

Common law

Private nuisance

At common law a person has a right of action against another for private nuisance if he has suffered unlawful interference with the use and enjoyment of his land. The interference caused by smoke, grit, dust, smells or fumes may involve damage to property or may be an interference with his ordinary comfort. The courts draw a distinction between actions in nuisance on the grounds of injury to property and those on grounds of personal discomfort.[1] Where the nuisance takes the form of interference with personal comfort or enjoyment, it must be of such degree that it is unreasonable, and in deciding what is unreasonable the court takes into account the character of the neighbourhood.[2] Remedy is by compensation and/or injunction.

Public nuisance

Anything 'which obstructs or causes inconvenience or damage to the public in the exercise of rights common to all Her Majesty's subjects'[3] may constitute a public nuisance. This is a crime, but if any person can prove that he has suffered particular damage, he has a right of action at civil law for compensation. This action in tort differs from private nuisance in that he need not show any interference with the use or enjoyment of land.

1   St Helen's Smelting *v* Tipping (1865) 11 H.L. Cas. 642.
2   'Whether anything is a nuisance or not is a question to be determined, not merely by an abstract consideration of the thing itself, but in reference to its circumstances; what would be a nuisance in Belgrave Square would not necessarily be so in Bermondsey.'— Thesiger L.J. in Sturgess *v* Bridgman (1879) 11 Ch.D. 856.
3   Sir J. F. Stephen, *Digest of Criminal Law*, Sweet & Maxwell, London, 1950.

Rule in Rylands v Fletcher

If a person creates increased danger by bringing onto or collecting on his land anything likely to be dangerous if it escapes, he must keep it in at his peril. Should it escape, even though there is no negligence on his part, he is liable for any damage that it does. Rylands v Fletcher[4] concerned the escape of water from a reservoir. In the course of his judgement Blackburn J. made it clear that he considered it applied also to a 'person . . . whose habitation is made unhealthy by the fumes and noisome vapours of his neighbour's alkali works',[5] and it can apply equally to dust, smuts, grit, fumes and gas.[6]

Its application to air pollution is limited, however, for as the rule has developed it is clear that there must be some non-natural use of the defendant's land. The exact meaning in this context of 'non-natural' is still open to dispute. In 1913 it was defined as 'some special use bringing with it increased dangers to others, and not merely the ordinary use of land or such use as is proper for the general benefit of the community',[7] while in 1947 Lord Parker added, 'I think that all the circumstances of the time and place and practice of mankind must be taken into consideration so that what might be regarded as non-natural may vary according to those circumstances'.[8]

The tendency in more recent times has been to accept a greater range of uses as natural, thereby limiting the scope of the term. The working of mines and minerals on land was found to be natural,[9] and it was doubted whether having a munitions factory on land in time of war was non-natural.[8] Presumably today many ordinary industrial processes would fall outside the scope of the rule.

Yet where a plaintiff might fail in Rylands v Fletcher, he might well succeed in nuisance or negligence.

4 (1866) L.R. 1 Ex. 265, affirmed (1868) L.R. 3 H.L. 330.
5 (1866) L.R. 1 Ex. at 280.
6 Halsey v Esso Petroleum [1961] 2 All E.R. 145, applied to acid smuts; Batchelor v Tunbridge Wells Gas Company (1901) 84 L.T. 765, gas likely to pollute water supplies; West v Bristol Tramways Company [1908] 2 K.B. 14, noxious gases or fumes.
7 Rickards v Lothian [1913] A.C. 263 at 280.
8 Read v Lyons [1947] A.C. 156.
9 Rouse v Gravelworks [1940] 1 K.B. 489.

Effect of the common law

As with all common law remedies, these have been ineffective
to prevent or contain pollution. The more so in the case of air
pollution, since in nuisance the court often must take into
account the character of the district where the smoke or the
fumes are emitted, and in the Rule in Rylands *v* Fletcher the
tending to construe the term 'non-natural' narrowly leaves less
room for its application in this field.

Statutes

Statutory nuisances

The Public Health Act, 1936, provides a special statutory procedure for dealing summarily with certain public nuisances.
They are the public nuisances specified by Act of Parliament
as 'statutory nuisances'. These include 'any dust or effluvia
caused by any trade, business, manufacture or process, and
being prejudicial to the health of or a nuisance to the inhabitants of the neighbourhood'.[10]

A local authority has a statutory duty to cause its district to
be inspected from time to time for statutory nuisances.[11] Any
person who suffers from a statutory nuisance may, of course,
report it to his local authority. If the authority is satisfied that
the nuisance exists it has a duty to take action to suppress it.

Under the statutory procedure the local authority first serves
an abatement notice, and if that is not complied with the person
accused may be summoned to appear before magistrates. The
magistrates may then fine him and make a nuisance order.[12]
There is an alternative procedure under which a person may
make a complaint direct to a magistrate.[13]

Dark smoke emitted from the chimney of a private dwelling,
furnace or industrial plant is a statutory nuisance.[14] The pro-

10 P.H.A., 1936. s. 92(1)(*d*).
11 P.H.A., 1936, s. 91.
12 P.H.A., 1963, s. 93.
13 P.H.A., 1963, s. 99. There is also provision for proceedings in the
   High Court: s. 100.
14 C.A.A., 1956, s. 16.

cedure for this nuisance is simplified in that there is no need to serve an abatement notice. Maximum fines are £10 and £5 per day if the offence continues.

Difficulties frequently arose in dealing with nuisances which had ceased to exist by the time the complaint had been investigated. The Public Health (Recurring Nuisances) Act, 1969, was therefore passed, empowering the local authority to send a prohibition notice where it is satisfied that a nuisance has occurred and is likely to recur on the same premises. If the nuisance then recurs the authority may complain to the magistrates, who may then make a nuisance order and impose a fine.

Legislation to control pollution from fires, furnaces, etc

Control of air pollution from chimneys, fires, industrial plant and similar sources is exercised by two different groups of people, acting under two distinct sets of legislative provisions. Local authorities enforce the Clean Air Acts, dealing with smoke, grit and dust; the alkali inspectorate exercises control over specified industries, dealing mainly with noxious or offensive gases. There is no overlap in the jurisdictions of these two kinds of authorities, although in practice there is ample co-operation. The legislative provisions under which they work show two different approaches to the pollution problem.

Control under the clean air legislation

Control under the Clean Air Acts is exercised by councils of boroughs, urban districts and rural districts, and in London by the London boroughs and the Common Council of the City of London. The Secretary of State for the Environment has powers under the Clean Air Act, 1968, to compel local authorities to establish smoke control areas.

Dark smoke. If dark smoke is emitted from the chimney of any building the occupier commits an offence.[15] This is an absolute offence, therefore proof of intent is not necessary—the Act

15 C.A.A., 1956, s. 1.

puts the onus on the occupier to ensure that dark smoke is not emitted. Certain defences are provided, including unforeseen failure of apparatus and the fact that suitable fuel is not available.[16]

Dark smoke includes soot, ash and grit emitted in the smoke,[17] and is 'dark' if it appears as dark as shade 2 on the Ringelman chart. The presence of visible constituents shows that combustion is incomplete, and indicates the presence of pollutants. Although invisibility does not guarantee that it is pollutant-free, legislation based on visible smoke can be enforced easily, and will probably be of value as long as fires and furnaces using solid fuels are used.

Section 19 of the Act extends this prohibition to vessels in ports, harbours and rivers, and the Clean Air Act, 1968, s. 1, to fires in the open industrial or trade premises, but with inadvertence as a defence.

Some flexibility is introduced into these provisions by granting power to the Minister to permit smoke from chimneys for limited periods, and smoke from fires in the open air when certain types of waste must be burned.[18]

Arrestment of dust and grit. The Acts provide that new furnaces shall not use certain fuels, nor fuels at higher than specified rates, unless fitted with plant approved by the local authority for arresting grit and dust.[19] The Minister is empowered also to make regulations to compel occupiers to measure and record emissions of grit and dust,[20] and to prescribe limits on the rates of emission.[21] It is an offence, however to fail to use any practicable means there may be to minimise the emission of grit or dust.

16 C.A.A.. 1956, s. 1(3).
17 C.A.A., 1956, s. 34(1).
18 See Dark Smoke (Permitted Period) Regulations, 1958, S.I. 1958 No. 498; Clean Air (Emission of Dark Smoke) (Exemption) Regulations, 1969, S.I. 1969 No. 1263.
19 C.A.A., 1956, s. 6; C.A.A., 1968, s. 3.
20 C.A.A., 1956, s 7; the Clean Air (Measurement of Grit and Dust from Furnaces) Regulations, 1971, S.I. 1971 No. 161.
21 C.A.A., 1968, s. 2; the Clean Air (Emission of Grit and Dust from Furnaces) Regulations, 1971, S.I. 1971 No. 162.

Fumes. The Clean Air Act, 1968, s. 7, empowers the Minister to extend by regulations certain provisions concerning the arrestment and rates of emission of grit and dust to fumes, but no such regulations have yet been made.

Height of chimneys. The height of chimneys is controlled under two provisions. The Clean Air Act, 1956, s. 10,[22] now applies only to chimneys other than those serving furnaces. The local authority must reject plans for such chimneys unless it is satisfied that the chimney will be of sufficient height to prevent, so far as practicable, the smoke, grit, dust or gases from being prejudicial to health, or a nuisance. Appeal lies to the Minister.

The Clean Air Act, 1968, s. 6, deals with furnaces serving chimneys. Where a new chimney has been constructed, or where the capacity of the furnace has been increased so as to bring it within the scope of the section, it is an offence to use the furnace unless the height of the chimney has been approved by the local authority.

Neither provision applies to a generating station of the electricity boards, and the Minister can by regulation exempt certain others.[23]

Section 6 of this Act of 1968 has been criticised as not applying to oil-fired furnaces ruled at less than $1\frac{1}{4}$ million B.t.u. per hour and coal-fired furnaces burning less than 100 lbs of coal per hour. The criticism is based on an assertion that some such furnaces are capable of emitting 3 lbs of sulphur dioxide per hour.[24]

Smoke from furnaces. The Clean Air Act, 1956, s. 3, prohibits the installation in any building of a furnace[25] unless it is, so far as practicable, capable of being operated continuously without emitting smoke when burning fuel of the type for which the furnace was designed.

22 As amended by C.A.A., 1968, s. 6(12).
23 See Clean Air (Height of Chimneys) (Exemption) Order, 1969, S.I. 1969, 411.
24 See J. F. Garner and R. K. Crow, *Clean Air—Law and Practice*, third edition, Shaw, London, 1969, p. 57.
25 Except furnaces for domestic purposes with maximum capacity of not more than 55,000 B.t.u./hr.

Plans and specifications may be submitted to the local authority, and if these are approved the furnace is deemed to comply with the requirements of the section.

The Minister is empowered to make regulations requiring installation of smoke density meters. These would give the boiler-house man early warning when excessive smoke is being emitted. No such regulations have yet been made.

Smoke control areas.   The system of designating smoke control areas was introduced to control and reduce the emission of smoke from both domestic and industrial buildings.

Under the system a local authority may, by order confirmed by the Minister,[26] declare the whole or part of its district to be a smoke control area.[27] Thereafter it is an offence for any smoke to be emitted from a chimney of any building in that area, subject to any exemptions or limitations in force.[28] It is a defence to show that the emission of smoke was not caused by the use of any fuel other than an authorised fuel. The local authority may limit the operation of the order to certain classes of buildings or exempt specified buildings or classes of buildings.[29] The Minister is also empowered to exempt any class of fireplace, and has done so by a series of orders.[30]

A person adapting existing premises to comply with an order can claim seven-tenths of the cost from the local authority, and the authority has a discretion to pay the whole or any part of the remainder. The Minister is in turn empowered to make an Exchequer grant to the authority. The effect of the provisions is that generally the occupier meets 30 per cent of the cost, the local authority 30 per cent and the Exchequer 40 per cent. In the case of houses owned by the local authority, it must meet 60 per cent of the cost but may pass on half of this in increased

26 The Minister will not confirm until satisfied by independent enquiry that a sufficient supply of suitable fuel is available to the area.
27 C.A.A., 1956, s. 11(1).
28 C.A.A., 1956, s. 11(2).
29 C.A.A., 1956. s. 11(3).
30 Smoke Control Areas (Exempted Fireplaces) Orders, S.I. 1957 No. 541; S.I. 1959 No. 1207; S.I. 1966 No. 217; S.I. 1969 No. 164. These orders and the circulars referring to them can be found in *The Encyclopedia of Public Health*, vol. 2.

rents.[31] Where the authority pays more than seven-tenths, as it may do in particular cases to relieve hardship, there is no Exchequer contribution to the voluntary payment.

Before confirming an order the Minister always ensures that there is a sufficient supply of smokeless fuel available to house-holders in the area. The local authority may also, with the consent of the Minister,[32] postpone the operation of an order.[33]

Government policy has for a long time been to encourage progress with smoke control, particularly in those parts of the country designated 'black areas'. Despite pressure from the government there is some resistance in certain areas, often in mining areas, where concessionary coal is received, and perhaps because of fear of unemployment if coal is no longer used.

Because progress under the 1956 Act was disappointing in some areas, by the 1968 Act the Minister was given power to direct a local authority to prepare and submit to him for his approval proposals for bringing into operation one or more orders.[34] This power has not yet been used, partly because of a temporary shortage of smokeless fuel, and in any case will be used only after persuasion has failed. Progress in 'black areas' is now about 5 per cent per annum.

Councillors clearly respond to public resistance to new smoke control orders. Individual councillors have often sounded out opinion in their wards and have found resistance on grounds of costs to individuals, particularly in wards with a high proportion of older or poorer people. This is, of course, the exercise of perfectly proper democratic control, and may be contrasted with the relationship between councillors and the general public in connection with the work of river authorities.

The enforcement of smoke control provisions in England and Wales is in the hands of local authorities. In 1968 there were 112 prosecutions under the Clean Air Acts as a whole, with 103 convictions, and fines in ninety-three cases. (See Appendix 2.)

31 See 'Memorandum on smoke control areas', Ministry of Housing and
   Local Government, circular 64/56, para. 18.
32 C.A.A., 1968, s. 10(2).
33 C.A.A., 1956, s. 11(6), and schedule 1, para. 6.
34 C.A.A., 1968, s. 8(1).

Redevelopment has helped progress. Building regulations[35] require that all new buildings shall be fitted with appliances capable of burning smokeless fuels. The use of planning powers has helped too, particular attention often being given to the siting of factories which may emit smoke.

Planning considerations, on the other hand, can conflict with pollution control. This frequently happens when chimney heights are considered, visual amenity conflicting with powers of dispersion. The conflict is usually settled by consultation between planning and public health departments and sometimes with the local alkali inspector, either because scheduled works are involved, or simply to give expert advice.[36] In nearly all cases, air pollution is the overriding consideration.

The Alkali, etc. Works Regulation Act, 1906

The first Alkali Act was passed in 1863 to control the emission of hydrochloric acid during the alkali manufacturing process. The scope of this legislation has been widened to cover the emission of certain 'noxious or offensive gases',[37] and the emission of smoke, grit and dust from processes within the jurisdiction of the alkali inspectorate.[38] This forms an entirely separate area of jurisdiction from that of the local authorities, but in practice there is ample co-operation between the local authority inspectors and the alkali inspectors.

The present Alkali Act covers alkali works, cement works and smelting works, and a long list of 'scheduled works'.[39] Power has been granted to the Secretary of State for the Environment to extend the schedule to cover other works.[40] Here is a centralised form of control exercised by the alkali inspectors, who are

35 S.I. 1965 No. 1373.
36 See 106th annual report of the Alkali Inspector, pp. 9–10.
37 These gases were first listed in A.A., 1906, s. 27(1). By powers granted under the Public Health (Smoke Abatement) Act, 1926, s. 4, and C.A.A., 1956, s. 17(3), this list has been extended. See now the Alkali, etc, Works Orders, 1966 and 1971, S.I. 1966 No. 1143, and S.I. 1971 No. 960.
38 C.A.A., 1968, s. 11(2).
39 See Alkali, etc, Works Order, 1966, S.I. 1966 No. 1143, as amended by the Alkali, etc, Works Order, 1971, S.I. 1971 No. 960.
40 Public Health (Smoke Abatement) Act, 1926, s. 4(1).

responsible to that Minister.[41] In the first place, no such work may be carried on unless registered, and it is a condition of registration that the works shall be furnished with such appliances as the Chief Inspector considers necessary for compliance with the Act.[41a]

Under ss. 1 and 6 fixed standards are laid down for certain classes of work releasing hydrochloric acid or sulphuric anhydride, and under s. 8 powers are given to fix standards for cement and smelting works. The standards fixed under ss. 1 and 6 are within safety limits, are easily maintained, and any excess is an indication of some fault at the works.

The provisions governing the other works are of much greater interest, for they provide a system under which the highest practicable standards can be maintained, and by which these standards can be raised in step with further technical advances.

Sections 2, 7 and 8(2)[42] provide that the owner shall use the best practicable means for preventing the escape of noxious or offensive gases, and for rendering such gases when discharged harmless and inoffensive.[43] The best practicable means is established after consultations between the Chief Alkali Inspector or one of his deputies and representatives of the industry concerned. A working party is formed and if necessary experimental work done within the works of member firms. This enables the Chief Alkali Inspector to establish the best practicable means for that industry and to issue a general direction to his inspectors. The district inspectors then relate this to the situation within their areas, and establish the requirements for individual firms.

The policy of the inspectorate was explained in the 1966 annual report of the Chief Inspector:

The ideals for which we strive are not achievable practically at the time decisions have to be taken, and one has to look back over the years to see how standards have improved with time, technical know-how and public demands. There will be no slackening in our

41 A.A., 1906, ss. 10–14.   41a A.A., 1906, s. 9.
42 A.A., 1906, subject to some provisional requirement in the case of cement and smelting works. See s. 8(1) and (2).
43 To which C.A.A., 1968, s. 11(2), has added smoke, grit and dust.

endeavours to achieve perfection, but practicable means have to be tempered to suit the times, and we shall continue to administer the Alkali Act in that helpful spirit which began with the first inspector and has continued ever since. This does not mean that we are soft with industry, for we firmly believe that more can be achieved by co-operation than by coercion, and that the inspectorate catalyses the modernisation of works processes ... Full 'best practicable means' is reached when the standard of emissions is so high as to result in little or no impact on the community and with no scope for further improvements ... There are some processes where the status of best practicable means has not yet been reached, and we usually refer to these as 'provisional best practicable means' whilst the full answers are being sought. In some provisional cases we are close to solutions and it is our contention not to delay their application to new plants when the answers are known ... In the absence of justified complaints, works which have installed provisional means will be allowed to operate their plants within their economic lines before measures which have been developed subsequently are demanded ... The expression 'best practicable means' takes into account economics in all its financial implications, and we interpret this not just in the narrow sense of a works dipping into its own pockets, but including the wider effect on the community.

Where a works does not use the best practicable means the owner is guilty of an offence.[44] He may on summary conviction be fined up to £100 and for a repetition or continuation of the offence up to £20 per day.[45]

Proceedings may be brought only by an inspector with the sanction of the Secretary of State. Criminal proceedings are very rare and in fact each application to prosecute has hitherto been considered personally by the Minister. If a local authority or the inhabitants of a local authority area complain of a contravention of the Act occasioning a nuisance, the Minister shall hold such enquiry and give such directions to the alkali inspector as he thinks fit and just.[46]

In practice the local alkali inspector responds to all apparently genuine complaints, seeing both the complainant and the factory management. There is considerable pressure from the public, press and interested associations, which has increased in recent years. As pressure increases, standards tend to improve.

44 Subject to the defence provided by s. 20.
45 C.A.A., 1956, s. 17(4) and schedule 2.
46 A.A., 1906. s. 22.

Control over a process by the alkali inspectorate is considered necessary, and therefore the process is placed on the list of scheduled works, whenever scientific or technical knowledge is needed for the exercise of proper control of emissions. Because of their special knowledge and competence, the advice of the alkali inspectors is frequently sought, and freely given, both at local and central government level. The two jurisdictions created by the Clean Air Acts and the Alkali Act are mutually exclusive, but there is full co-operation between those who administer them.

There is also provision[47] for a local authority to apply to the Secretary of State for an order transferring jurisdiction over emissions of smoke, grit and dust from the whole or any specified part of any work from the alkali inspectorate to the local authority. In prosecutions relating to emissions of smoke, however, the occupier of the works retains the defence that the best practicable means was employed to prevent or minimise the emission.[47]

At the public enquiry which preceded issue of the Alkali, etc, Works Order, 1971,[48] it became clear that when a process gives rise to many local complaints the local authority prefers to keep that process within its jurisdiction. An order under s. 11 can ensure that it does. It is quite clear that, even though a district alkali inspector always takes into account a complaint by a local authority,[49] some councils do not feel that this is sufficient. This does not necessarily mean a lack of faith in the alkali inspectorate; it may mean that local conditions or localised effects of the works emissions justify the application of a separate local standard by locally elected representatives. It is, of course, for the Secretary of State to decide whether or not a transfer of jurisdiction is justified.

Exhaust smoke from motor vehicles

The present law concerns itself only with smoke and visible

---

47 C.A.A., 1968, s. 11(3).
48 Public enquiry on proposed Alkali Order, 28 October 1970
49 The matter may also be referred to the Secretary of State for enquiry. See p. 65 *supra*.

emissions from motor vehicles. This law is found in the Construction and Use Regulations, 1969, and, as may well be
expected, covers both the construction and the use of the
vehicle.

Regulation 24 requires that every motor vehicle shall be so
constructed that no avoidable smoke or vapour is emitted therefrom.[50] Regulation 84 requires that no person shall use or cause
or permit to be used on a road any motor vehicle from which
any smoke, visible vapour, grit, ashes, sparks, cinders, or oily
substance is emitted if the emission causes or is likely to cause
damage to any property or injury or danger to any person who
is on or may be expected to be on the road.

Annual tests of motor vehicles do not require compliance
with these regulations, but under the Road Traffic Act, 1960,
s. 67,[51] an authorised examiner may test a vehicle on the road to
ascertain whether or not, *inter alia*, these regulations are satisfied. A vehicle shall not be required to stop for a test except by
a police constable in uniform. 'Authorised examiner' for this
purpose includes a police constable authorised so to act by or
under the instructions of the chief officer of police.[52] The driver
may elect to defer the examination, except where an accident
has occurred and 'it is requisite that the test be carried out
forthwith'.

Certain goods vehicles must be submitted to annual tests
under the Goods Vehicles (Plating and Testing) Regulations,
1968. The test is to ensure, *inter alia*, that the vehicle may be
used so as not to emit smoke, etc, as required by regulation 84
above.

A recent amendment to the regulations applies to all motor
vehicles propelled by spark ignition engines, other than two-
strokes, first used on or after 1 January 1971. The vehicle will
have to be so equipped as to ensure that vapours or gases are
prevented from escaping from the crankcase into the atmosphere, and this equipment will have to be maintained in good

50 Other relevant regulations are regulation 25, relating to compression
   ignition engines, and regulation 26, relating to motor vehicles using
   solid fuel.
51 As amended by R.T.A., 1962, schedule 4.
52 R.T.A., 1960, s. 67(2).

working order while the vehicle is used on the road.[53]

Regulations at present in force governing the emission of smoke and visible vapour from motor vehicles are enforced by the police. The attention of the officer is usually attracted by a noisy exhaust, and a prosecution may be brought for both emission of smoke and visible vapour and for excessive noise. The police experience no difficulty in enforcing this very limited degree of control. In 1968 prosecutions numbered 777, leading to 754 convictions.[54]

53 Motor Vehicles (Construction and Use) (Amendment) Regulations, 1971, S.I. 1971 No. 444.
54 See Appendix 2 for figures for more recent years.

5 Nuclear energy

Pollution may occur as a result of the disposal of atomic waste, or an accidental emission of ionising particles. Safeguards to prevent such occurrences lie in close Ministerial controls over the operation of nuclear installations, and over the keeping, use and disposal of radioactive materials.

Control of nuclear installations and operations

The Secretary of State for Trade and Industry has power of control over the Atomic Energy Authority. He may, after consultation with the A.E.A., give directions to it, but not in detail unless in his opinion overriding national interests so require.[1] Other government departments carrying out work in the field of nuclear energy are under the control of the relevant Ministers.

Other persons wishing to use a site for installing or operating a nuclear reactor, or any other installation which is designed or adapted for, *inter alia*, the storage, processing or disposal of nuclear fuel or bulk quantities of radioactive matter, must obtain a nuclear site licence from the Minister.[2] A site licence is issued only to a corporate body and is not transferable.

Where the Minister receives an application for a site licence, he may direct the applicant to serve a notice on the following authorities:

1. Any local authority.
2. Any river authority, local fisheries committee or statutory water undertaker.
3. Any other body which is a public authority.

The notice shall state that the application has been made, shall include such particulars as may be specified by the Minister with

1   A.E.A. Act, 1954, s. 3(1).
2   N.I.A., 1965, s. 1.

respect to the use of the proposed site, and state that representations may be made to the Minister within three months of the
service of notice.[3] The Central Electricity Generating Board is
exempt from this provision as to notice, but the Board must
always gain the consent of the Minister for the building of any
generating station, and there is adequate provision for notifica-
tion of parties who might be affected.

On granting the licence the Minister is bound to attach such
conditions as appear to him to be necessary or desirable in the
interests of safety, and may from time to time thereafter attach
further conditions. These conditions may include provision for:

(a) Maintenance of a system of detecting and recording ionising
radiations from anything on the site or discharged from the site.

(b) Preparations for dealing with, and measures to be taken on
the happening of an accident or other emergency on the site.

(c) Discharge of any substance on or from the site, without
prejudice to authorisations under the Radioactive Substances Act,
1960, ss. 6 and 8.[4]

The Minister may also impose such conditions as he thinks fit
in respect of handling, treatment and the disposal of nuclear
matter.[5]

In practice, before any application for a site licence is formally
submitted, there is informal discussion between the prospective
candidate and the Chief Inspector of Nuclear Installations. A
licence is first granted with general conditions, but when the
detailed designs and proposed operating procedures have been
examined, permission to operate plant is given subject to further
requirements. While a site licence remains in force, the Minister
must consider any representations made to him by any organ-
isations representing persons having duties upon the site with a
view to exercising his power to impose further conditions.[6] The
section does not, however, extend to other representative organ-
isations such as river authorities and fisheries committees.

The Minister has appointed a nuclear installations inspectorate. Any inspector may enter and inspect a licensed site,

3   N.I.A., 1965, s. 3.
4   N.I.A., 1965, s. 4(1).
5   N.I.A., 1965, s. 4(2).
6   N.I.A., 1965, s. 4(4).

inspect documents and require information. Penalties for installing or operating without a site licence, and for breach of any
condition, are a fine of £100 and/or three months' imprisonment
on summary conviction, and £500 and/or five years' on indictment. The Minister may at any time revoke a licence.

Civil liabilities of operators of nuclear installations

Although an operator could undoubtedly have been made liable
at common law in many circumstances for damage or injuries
resulting from discharge of nuclear waste or from a nuclear
accident, the Nuclear Installations Act, 1965, imposes a liability
which is more strict and wider in its scope. There is therefore
nothing to be gained from examining the common law.

The object of the legislation appears to be to ensure that the
operator takes all precautions to prevent injury or damage, even
to the extent of safeguarding against natural disasters and
intermeddling by other persons. He is absolved only in the
event of acts done by the plaintiff recklessly or with the intention of causing harm, and of course damage attributable to
hostile action in the course of armed conflict. The provisions
apply to site licences, the A.E.A., and to government departments installing or operating nuclear installations.[7] For the sake
of brevity the term 'operator' is used in the following paragraphs
to cover all these.

The operator is under a duty to secure that no occurrence
involving nuclear matter causes injury to the person or damage
to the property of another. He is liable if the occurrence takes
place on his site, in course of carriage on his behalf, in course of
carriage to his site from certain overseas territories, and else-
where than on his site if it has not, broadly speaking, become
the responsibility of another operator.[8] He is also under a duty
to secure that no ionising radiations are emitted, *inter alia*, from
any waste discharged on or from the site so as to cause injury
to the person or damage to the property of another.[9]

'Damage to property' is a term wide enough to cover damage

7   N.I.A., 1965, ss. 8 and 9.
8   N.I.A., 1965, s. 7(1) and (2).
9   N.I.A., 1965, s. 7(1).

to private fishing rights. Where, however, there is a public right to fish, no property is involved. Even the fish do not become the property of the fisherman until they are caught. If, therefore, owners of sea-going trawlers find their profits fall as a result of discharge of atomic waste, there is no right of action under the Act.[10] If the damage is done within the three-mile limit, there may be a right of action for public nuisance, but outside that limit there would be no right of action at common law.

The liabilities of any operation arising out of any one occurrence are limited to £5 million.[11] Each operator is to make provision, by insurance or otherwise, as the Minister with the consent of the Treasury approves, to meet such a claim.[12]

No action may be entertained after a period of thirty years from the date of an occurrence involving nuclear material, and in the case of nuclear material lost, jettisoned or abandoned, after a period of twenty years.[13]

If a claim is not met because the limitation period has expired, or not met in full because of the limitation on the liability of the operator, a claim may be made to the appropriate Minister. The Minister may then satisfy the claim to such extent and out of funds provided by such means as Parliament may determine.[14] A claimant under this section must first satisfy the Minister, and is then dependent on the will of Parliament to make provision to satisfy his claim. The Act further provides that there shall be a fund provided by Parliament to ensure that claims are satisfied up to an aggregate of £43 million.[15]

Where an operator is liable under one of the foregoing sections, no other liability shall be incurred by any other person for that injury or damage. This fixes liability solely on the operator, even to the extent of preventing him from having recourse to others who might otherwise have been liable.

10 See H. Street and F. R. Frame, *Law Relating to Nuclear Energy*, Butterworth, London, 1966, p. 55.
11 N.I.A., 1965, s. 16(1).
12 N.I.A., 1965, s. 19. And see ss. 16(3) and 18 below for provisions covering cases where the operator does not meet the claim in full.
13 N.I.A., 1965, s. 15(1) and (2).
14 N.I.A., 1965, s. 16(3).
15 N.I.A., 1965, s. 18.

Control of radioactive substances

Controls over dealings in, and the use, carriage and disposal of, radioactive substances were introduced by the Radioactive Substances Act, 1948. Section 2 granted power to the Minister of Supply to prohibit or regulate the import, export and carriage coastwise of any radioactive substances. Section 5 granted power to 'the appropriate Ministers'[16] to make regulations, *inter alia*, to ensure that radioactive waste products are disposed of safely. This power has not been used, and it is unlikely that it will be now that closer control has been provided for by the Act of 1960.

The Radioactive Substances Act, 1960,[17] first provides for the registration of all persons keeping or using, or knowingly permitting to be kept or used, on any premises any radioactive material.[18] Registration is with the Secretary of State for the Environment, who may impose such limitations and conditions as he thinks fit. The A.E.A. is exempt from registration,[19] and site licensees are exempt, but the Minister may impose limitations and conditions on them.[20] The Minister may grant further exemptions from registration by reference to classes of premises and undertakings and descriptions of radioactive materials,[21] but again he may impose limitations and conditions.

The Act then provides that no person shall dispose of, or cause or permit to be disposed of, any radioactive waste except in accordance with an authorisation granted by the Secretary of State for the Environment.[22] The Minister has power to grant exemptions similar to those powers in respect of registration.[23] No person shall accumulate, or cause or permit to be accumulated, any radioactive waste on his premises, except in accord-

16 It is provided that these may be designated by order in council.
17 Passed largely as a result of recommendations in *The Control of Radioactive Wastes*, Cmnd. 884.
18 Section 1.
19 Section 2(1).
20 Section 2(2) and (3).
21 A large number of exemption orders have been made.
22 Sections 6 and 7. In the case of the A.E.A. and site licensees, authorisation must be granted by the Secretary of State for the Environment and the Minister of Agriculture, Fisheries and Food jointly.
23 Section 6(5).

ance with an authorisation.[24] In this case the A.E.A. and nuclear site licensees are exempt.

Authorisations may be granted in respect of waste generally or for waste of a specified class.[25] It is through the requirements laid down by authorisation that the control is exercised.

The Act, moreover, provides for consultation with other public authorities who may be affected. Before authorisation is granted for disposal from premises of the A.E.A. or a site licensee, each of the two Ministries must consult the local authorities, local fisheries committees, statutory water undertakers and other local or public authorities they consider proper to be consulted.[26] Also, in any case in which disposal is likely to involve special precautions by such authorities, they must first be consulted by the Minister or Ministers.[27] If special precautions are taken, the person disposing of the waste may be charged with expenses involved as provided in s. 9(4).

The authorisation to dispose of waste may require or permit it to be removed to a place provided by local authorities. In such case it is the duty of the local authority to accept the waste.[28] Alternatively, if the Minister thinks that adequate facilities for disposal or accumulation are not available, he may provide them.

The Minister may appoint inspectors who have the usual rights of entry and inspection. The Act does not apply to the Crown, nor to any government department or visiting forces.

Control over radioactive substances is kept exclusively with the relevant Ministers, for s. 10 of the 1960 Act provides that no account shall be taken of radioactivity for the purposes of the following provisions:

Sea Fisheries Regulation Acts.
Salmon and Freshwater Fisheries Act, 1923, ss. 8 and 59.
Certain Sections of the Public Health Act, 1936.
Public Health (Drainage of Trade Premises) Act, 1937.
Rivers (Prevention of Pollution) Act, 1951.
Clean Air Act, 1956.

24 Section 7.   25 Section 8(4).
26 Section 8(7).   27 Section 9(3).
28 Section 9(5).

The National Radiological Protection Board

The Radiological Protection Act, 1970, established for the first time an independent advisory body known as the National Radiological Protection Board.[29] The Board consists of a chairman and seven to nine other members. All are appointed by the 'Health Ministers'[30] after consultation with the A.E.A. and Medical Research Council. There is also a statutory advisory committee comprising the chairman of the Board and fourteen to twenty-four other members appointed by the Health Ministers.

These members represent a wide range of interests, including the professions, government departments with statutory responsibility for radiological protection, the T.U.C., the C.B.I. and other interested associations. This committee will thus be a representative body, but also will inevitably include men with relevent professional and technical qualifications.

The duties of the Board are:[31]

1. To advance the acquisition of knowledge about the protection of mankind from radiation hazards.
2. To provide information and advice to persons, including government departments, with responsibilities in the U.K. in relation to radiation hazards.
3. To advise any Minister who has functions under the Radioactive Substances Acts.
4. In accordance with directions given by the Health Ministers, assume responsibilities for the Radiological Protection Service and carry on, in place of the A.E.A., activities related to the effect of radiation hazards on health and safety.

The Board has power to provide technical services.[32]

There are special features in the control of pollution from radioactive sources which are not found in the case of pollutants from other sources. In the first place the scientific work is highly specialised and beyond the competence of the staff of

29 Section 2.
30 These are: the Secretary of State for the Social Services, the Secretary of State for Scotland, the Secretary of State for Wales, and the Minister of Health and Social Services for Northern Ireland.
31 See s. 1(1), (5) and (3), and R.S.A., 1948, s. 6.
32 Section 1(2).

most public authorities. In the second place the number of firms handling radioactive substances in a way which might lead to pollution of the environment is small. Therefore a system of licensing and direct control by a central authority is possible. Given adequate inspection and monitoring, this is probably the most effective form of control.

Any risks involving the general public can now be brought to the attention of the responsible Minister by an independent body, the Board, and the Board in turn is advised by a committee that is in some degree representative. Furthermore, those concerned with radiological protection work well within the limits established by the International Commission on Radiological Protection.

6 Noise

Common law

Noise, like the emission of smoke or fumes, can be a private or public nuisance.[1]

Noise as a statutory nuisance

The Noise Abatement Act, 1960, s. 1 provides that noise or vibration which is a nuisance shall be a statutory nuisance. To be a nuisance in law it must be sufficient to give grounds for a right of action at common law;[1] the statutory procedure of the Public Health Act, 1936, can then be invoked.[2] Under the alternative procedure of complaint direct to a magistrate, in the case of noise or vibration complaint must be made by at least three persons, each of whom must be the occupier of land or premises and in that capacity aggrieved.[3] This rule was introduced because of the subjective nature of the complaint. Thus the complainant must satisfy the local authority that the noise constitutes a nuisance, or find two other occupiers of land or premises to join in the complaint, or proceed with a civil action on his own behalf. The Public Health (Recurring Nuisances) Act, 1969, has done much to render the statutory procedure more effective in the cases of noise nuisances.[4]

If the noise or vibration is caused in the course of trade or business, it is a defence to prove that the best practicable means have been used for preventing and counteracting its effect.[5] In deciding whether the best practicable means have been used, the

1 See section 4, 'Air pollution', under 'Common law'. See also Halsey *v* Esso Petroleum [1961] 2 All E.R. 145.
2 See section 4, 'Air pollution', under 'Statutory Nuisances'.
3 N.A.A., 1960, s. 1(2).
4 See p. 58 *supra*.
5 N.A.A., 1960, s. 1(3).

court has regard to the cost and to local conditions and circumstances. There is an exemption in favour of statutory undertakers,[6] and almost complete exemption in favour of aircraft.[7]

The Noise Abatement Act, 1960, s. 2 places prohibitions on
the use in the street of loudspeakers. No loudspeaker may be
operated in the street at any time for the purpose of advertising,
entertainment, trade or business, except that between 12.00 noon
and 7.00 p.m. the sale of perishable food may be so advertised,
provided the use of the speaker does not cause an annoyance.
Other exemptions are granted under sub-section (2).

Bye-laws

Every county council and borough council is empowered to make
bye-laws for the good rule and government of its area, and for
the prevention and suppression of nuisances.[8] This gives wide
powers to suppress nuisance by noise. The bye-laws are subject
to confirmation by the relevant Minister, and even if so approved
can be declared invalid by the court if unreasonable.

Aircraft

The effect of the Civil Aviation Act, 1949, is to take away from
members of the public all rights to sue in nuisance for noise and
vibration caused by the normal and proper operation of aircraft,
and to put into the hands of the Secretary of State powers of
regulation.

Under s. 8 the Crown is empowered to make provision by
orders in council for regulating air navigation generally, and in
particular for prohibiting aircraft from flying over such areas in
the United Kingdom as may be specified in the order, and specifying the conditions under which, and the aerodromes to or from
which, aircraft entering or leaving the United Kingdom may fly.

Section 41 empowers the Crown also to make provision for
regulating the conditions under which noise and vibration may
be caused by aircraft on aerodromes.

6   N.A.A., 1960, s. 1(4).
7   See under 'Aircraft' *infra*
8   L.G.A., 1933, s. 249.

The counterparts to these provisions lie in ss. 40(1) and 41(2). The former provides that no action shall lie in respect of trespass or nuisance by reason only of the flight of aircraft over any property at a height above ground which, having regard to wind, weather and all the circumstances of the case, is reasonable, or in the ordinary incidents of such flight so long as the statutory provisions governing flight, including orders in council made under s. 8, are observed. The latter section provides that no action shall lie in respect of nuisance by reason only of the noise and vibration caused by aircraft on an aerodrome to which an order in council under s. 8 applies,[9] so long as the provisions of the order are observed.

The Air Navigation Order, 1966,[10] empowers the Secretary of State to prescribe conditions under which noise and vibration may be made by aircraft on government aerodromes, licensed aerodromes and aerodromes at which the repair or maintenance of aircraft is carried out as a business. These powers have been exercised by the Air Navigation General Regulations, 1966, S.I. 1966 No. 1256.

Certain classes of aircraft having turbojet or turbofan engines require a noise certificate before they can take off from or land at any airport in the United Kingdom.[11]

Under the Airports Authority Act, 1965, Heathrow, Gatwick, Stansted and Prestwick airports have been transferred to a corporate body, the British Airports Authority, the chairman and members of which are appointed by the Secretary of State.[12] There is also provision for acquiring other airports. Section 14 of the Act gives the Secretary of State power to require the Authority to take such measures as he shall direct for limiting noise and vibration or mitigating their effect and for restricting the use of the airport. If the Secretary of State considers that further protection is needed for dwellings near an airport owned or managed by the Authority, he may draw up a scheme requiring

9 See Air Navigation Order, 1966, *infra.*
10 S.I. 1966 No. 1184, Art. 68; also Colonial Air Navigation Order, 1961, S.I. 1961 No. 2316, Art. 68.
11 Air Navigation (Noise Certification) Order, 1970, S.I. 1970 No. 823.
12 Airports Authority Act, 1965, s. 1.

the Authority to make grants towards the cost of installing noise insulation in those dwellings.[13]

In 1967 the Parliamentary Commissioner dealt with a complaint that the Board of Trade, as the responsible department, was failing to control effectively the noise caused by air traffic using Heathrow Airport. He accepted that it was within his jurisdiction to investigate such a complaint. His report[14] exonerated the Board.

A number of airports remain vested in local authorities. In those cases the Secretary of State hitherto has had no powers to give directions. He has, of course, been able to use his powers under the Air Navigation Order, 1966, but beyond this, the use and development of the airport lie with the local authority. There are many local considerations to be taken into account, such as the location of private dwellings and, in particular, sensitive areas such as hospital buildings. For example, Cheadle Royal Hospital is situated only $1\frac{1}{2}$ miles from one of the runways of Manchester Airport. Manchester Airport Committee take this into account when considering noise abatement measures such as restricting the number of night jet movements, determining flight paths and specifying preferential take-off directions.

A council owning or managing an airport naturally has an interest in developing a thriving airport; on the other hand, the increase in traffic can cause considerable noise nuisance. Where the residents affected by the noise are electors of that local government, the council is subject to the normal political pressures. In some cases, however, the people affected live in a different local authority area. Although planning restrictions and the Secretary of State's general powers provide some safeguard for them, they remain at comparative disadvantage, being unable to exert any political pressure on the council which controls the airport.

The government is aware of the problem of noise at airports, and particularly at municipal airports. In the debate on the

13 He has done so in the case of Heathrow by the London (Heathrow) Airport Noise Insulation Grants Scheme, 1966, S.I. 1966 No. 424.
14 Second report of the Parliamentary Commissioner for Administration, session 1967–68.

second reading of the civil aviation Bill (now the Civil Aviation Act, 1971) the Under-Secretary for Trade and Industry said,[15]

It is because the government have a duty to maintain a balance between the interests of the industry and the amenity of the public that the main responsibility for noise abatement cannot be given to the Authority (the new Civil Aviation Authority) but must remain with the government.

He later stated,[16]

The government have no powers at present to impose noise abatement measures at municipally or private owned aerodromes. I recognise the considerable interest in this aspect which is under review. However, the separation of responsibility for noise from the responsibilities of ownership raises a number of very difficult legal and financial problems with which it would not be appropriate to deal with in this Bill.

Nevertheless the Act does contain provisions giving the Secretary of State for Trade and Industry further powers to control noise and vibration caused by landing and take off at all airports. He may publish a notice designating any aerodrome in Great Britain, and specify requirements to be complied with before an aircraft lands or after it has taken off. It will then be the duty of the operator of the aircraft to secure compliance.[17] If he fails to do so, the facilities for using the aerodrome may be withheld from the aircraft and the servants of the operator.[18]

For the same purposes, the Secretary of State may limit the number of occasions on which aircraft may land at or take off from a designated aerodrome during certain periods. He may publish a notice specifying the periods, and the maximum number of occasions for each particular class of aircraft.[19]

He may also give to any person managing an aerodrome in Great Britain directions for limiting or mitigating the effect of noise and vibration at landing or take-off.[20] He may furthermore require noise measuring equipment to be installed and reports to be submitted on the noise measured.[21]

15 Hansard, vol. 184, col. 1177.
16 *Ibid.*, col. 1178.
17 Civil Aviation Act, 1971, s. 29(1).
18 Civil Aviation Act, 1971, s. 29(2).
19 Civil Aviation Act, 1971, s. 29(3).
20 Civil Aviation Act, 1971, s. 29(5).
21 Civil Aviation Act, 1971, s. 29(7).

The provisions of the Act are to come into force on days to be appointed. Until a technical solution can be found to the problem of aircraft noise, it lies with the government to try to maintain some balance between the interest of operators and the people they serve on the one hand, and public amenity on the other. The longer-term, and perhaps even more difficult, problem to be faced is how much in money and resources can the aircraft industry, and perhaps the government, reasonably be expected to commit to research and development and higher production costs in building quieter aircraft. But this is an economic aspect of the pollution problem to be examined in a subsequent volume in this series.

Motor vehicles

The law governing noise from motor vehicles is to be found in the Construction and Use Regulations, 1969.[22]

Every vehicle must be fitted with an audible warning instrument,[23] but subject to certain exceptions gongs, bells, sirens and two-tone horns are forbidden. The instrument must not be sounded when the vehicle is stationary on any road, or moving along a restricted road between 11.30 p.m. and 7.30 a.m.,[24] although the regulation contains numerous exceptions.

Every vehicle must be fitted with a silencer,[25] and, subject to certain exceptions, must be so constructed that the noise from the vehicle does not exceed certain specified sound levels.[26]

Regulations 87 and 88 require that no motor vehicle which causes an excessive noise shall be used on a road, nor any motor vehicle used on a road in such a manner as to cause excessive noise which could have been avoided by the exercise of reasonable care.

More specific limitations are laid down in regulation 89, under which it is an offence to use a motor vehicle on any road so as to exceed certain specified sound levels.

22 S.I. 1969 No. 321.
23 Regulation 21(1).
24 Regulation 91(1).
25 Regulation 22.
26 Regulation 23.

Annual testing of cars in no way relates to noise, but vehicles may be stopped on the road and tested for compliance with the regulations as to silencers under the Road Traffic Act, s. 67.[27] The Goods Vehicles (Plating and Testing) Regulations, 1968, apply to silencers as they do to exhaust smoke.

The noise regulation governing the construction of the vehicle[28] is directed at the relatively few manufacturers and importers, and so is not difficult to enforce; but regulation 89 governing the use of the vehicle on the road is regarded by the police as unenforceable. That is not surprising. The conditions under which the test is to be made are specified in schedule 10 of the regulations. They are reproduced in Appendix 1. It is obvious that the police cannot carry out such a test in an urban area and be able to present a 'water-tight' case in court. Even in a rural area, conditions such as those laid down in the schedule must still create many difficulties for the police, and many opportunities for the defence advocate.

This is not a case of the police abdicating from their responsibilities. They are merely refusing to attempt what is virtually impossible. They do, on the other hand, enforce regulations 87 and 88, which prohibit excessive noise from motor vehicles.[29]

In a typical case the police officer's attention will first be attracted by excessive noise from a defective silencer. He may decide to prosecute under regulation 82(2) for a faulty silencer. If a charge is brought under 87 and 88 oral evidence will be given by the officer, backed by evidence as to the physical state of the silencer. A prosecution would not be brought on evidence of noise alone.

The enforcement of fixed standards for noise emissions from motor vehicles throughout their periods of use on the roads presents considerable difficulties. In some European countries[30] police can stop a vehicle they consider is making excessive noise and require the driver to submit to a test at an official testing station, but with no punishment if any defect has been remedied in the meantime. Similar requirements are contem-

27 See Section 4, 'Air pollution', under 'Motor vehicles'.
28 Regulation 23 referred to *supra*.
29 For the number of prosecutions and convictions see Appendix 2.
30 E.g. France, the Netherlands.

plated for this country. It is not entirely satisfactory, however, if motorists feel able to carry on in breach of the regulations, knowing that they can escape liability by remedying the defect after they have been stopped.

Planning powers and the regulations of noise

Local authorities are keenly aware of the nuisance created by excessive noise from premises, particularly from factories and clubs, and of recent years have become more concerned with the noise from busy roads. They rightly decide that prevention *ab initio* is the best remedy, and therefore take noise into account with applications for planning permission.

Where the application is to build a factory, or for a change of use to some industrial process, noise is not normally the first consideration, and if the siting of the factory is in other respects satisfactory, there will not usually be a refusal solely on the grounds of noise. The planning authority may instead impose conditions. Conditions imposing fixed noise limits are rarely used because of difficulties in enforcement. The authority may require a certain type of structure, such as a brick wall instead of asbestos sheeting, or may impose restrictions on the type of plant which may be used.

The difficulty in exercising control through planning powers is that there may be a change in practice which still falls within the same use class. Once excessive noise is made without breach of planning permission, the local authority is left to proceed for statutory nuisance.

Noise is now being given far greater consideration in the planning of urban highways, particularly urban motorways, than in the past. Naturally, careful route planning is of first importance but some reduction of noise effect can be obtained by screening. Trees and shrubs add to the visual merits of a scheme but do not form a very effective noise screen. Building the road in a cutting gives a greater reduction in noise effect but is highly expensive. Some countries have general guidelines for planners which specify minimum distances between highways and certain types of buildings.[31]

31 E.g. France, the Netherlands, Norway and Sweden.

These planning considerations form too large and complex a subject for discussion here. It is sufficient to note that, whilst good planning can usually help to minimise pollution problems, with noise pollution it is of particular importance, in view of the difficulty of enforcing legislation which attempts to limit noise levels.

7   Pollution of the sea by oil

The principal sources of oil pollution of the sea are accidents to tankers, the discharge of oily bilge water and the deliberate discharge of sea water which has been used as ballast or for washing out oil cargo tanks. Ships which have discharged their cargoes and are setting out on the return voyage take on sea water as ballast. Dry cargo ships use fuel tanks for this ballast water; oil tankers use empty cargo tanks. Oil tankers also used to take this opportunity to wash out their cargo tanks with sea water. The resulting oily mixture from these operations was discharged into the sea.

Following the publication of the Faulkner report,[1] the British government convened a conference in London to seek an agreed solution to this problem. An agreement was reached in 1954, and amended in 1962, and is known as the International Convention for the Prevention of Pollution of the Sea by Oil.

The Convention sought first to encourage provision for the separation of oil from water on sea-going ships, and the provision of facilities at ports for taking the oily residues when the ships arrived; then it sought to prohibit the disharge of oily mixtures into certain zones of the sea. Because no State has jurisdiction over the high seas, each signatory State can legislate only for its own territorial waters, and for its own ships, wherever they may be. If signatory States give mutual assistance in enforcing each other's legislation, and if all the major maritime States are signatories, this should give adequate control.

Extensive 'prohibited zones' have been established, and most maritime countries now provide facilities at their ports for the reception of oily residues.[2] The United Kingdom legislation

1 Ministry of Transport. *Report of the Committee on Pollution of the Sea by Oil*, H.M.S.O., London, 1953.
2 See *Facilities in Ports for the Reception of Oil Residues*. Results of an enquiry made in 1963 by I.M.C.O.

passed as a result of the 1954 Convention and the 1962 Amendment is outlined below.

The law in force is found mainly in the Oil in Navigable Waters Acts, 1955 and 1963, and in the regulations made thereunder.[3] This legislation is based on the International Convention for Oil Pollution Damage, 1954, as amended 1962, and is complemented by corresponding legislation of the other signatory States. These statutes have now been consolidated, with the Oil in Navigable Waters Act, 1971, and the Continental Shelf Act, 1964, s. 5, in the Prevention of Oil Pollution Act, 1971. The consolidating Act is to be brought into force on such dates as the Secretary of State shall appoint.

Territorial waters

An offence is committed where any oil or mixture containing oil is discharged into U.K. territorial waters, or any U.K. waters navigable by sea-going ships, from any vessel, from any place or land, or from a vessel transferring oil to or from land or another vessel. This applies to vessels irrespective of nationality or flag,[4] but the Secretary of State may exempt any vessels or classes of vessels.[5] Certain limited defences are provided in cases where the discharge was the result of damage or leakage.[6]

Prohibited sea areas

If any oil is discharged from a British ship registered in the U.K. in any prohibited sea area, the owner or master is guilty of an offence,[7] subject to special defences provided by s. 4 of the 1955 Act. Prohibited areas include all the seas round the British

---

3 A useful summary of legal prohibitions and requirements is to be found in the Board of Trade *Manual on the avoidance of Pollution of the Sea by Oil*, third edition, H.M.S.O., London, 1967, appendix 1.
4 O.N.W.A., 1955, s. 3; O.N.W.A., 1971. s. 2; P.O.P.A., 1971, s. 2.
5 O.N.W.A., 1955, s. 15; P.O.P.A., 1971, s. 23.
6 O.N.W.A., 1955, s. 4; O.N.W.A., 1971, s. 3; P.O.P.A., 1971, s. 5.
7 O.N.W.A., 1955, s. 1, as amended by O.N.W.A., 1963. O.N.W.A., 1971, s. 1, and P.O.P.A., 1971, s. 1, will prohibit discharges into any part of the sea outside the territorial waters of the United Kingdom, subject to any regulations made by the Secretary of State under P.O.P.A., 1971, s. 3, which may exclude particular areas.

Isles and a large stretch of the north Atlantic ocean.[8] The
Minister may extend these areas if he considers it necessary to
do so for the purpose of protecting the coasts and territorial
waters of the U.K. Defences relating to damage and leakage are
again available.

Every British ship registered in the U.K. is required to carry
an oil record book, in which details of all discharges, transfers
of oil to other ships, and other specified matters must be
entered.[9] Provision is made for inspection by authorised persons.

All sea areas

If any British ship of 20,000 tons or more registered in the U.K.
for which the building contract was made on or after 18 May
1967 discharges oil anywhere at sea, the owner or master is
guilty of an offence.[10] It is a defence to show that by reason of
special circumstances it was impracticable or unreasonable to
retain the oil on the ship.

The Minister is empowered to make regulations requiring
British ships registered in the U.K. to install equipment to prevent oil pollution.[11] Harbour authorities in the United Kingdom
are also empowered to provide facilities for enabling vessels to
discharge oil residues,[12] and the Minister may direct any harbour
authority to provide such facilities.[13]

Effect of present legislation

Forty-two countries are signatories to the oil Convention, covering 99 per cent of the tankers afloat, yet there is evidence that it
has been largely ineffective. It has reduced the spillage of oil

8 O.N.W.A., 1955, schedule 1, as amended. A map of the prohibited
   areas is to be found in the Board of Trade pamphlet mentioned in
   note 3 above.
9 O.N.W.A., 1955, s. 7; P.O.P.A., 1971, s. 17.
10 O.N.W.A., 1963, s. 2; see now P.O.P.A., 1971, s. 1.
11 Two sets of regulations are now in force: the Oil in Navigable
   Waters (Ships' Equipment) Regulations, 1956, S.I. 1956 No. 1423,
   and S.I. 1957 No. 1424.
12 O.N.W.A., 1955, s. 8(1); P.O.P.A., 1971, s. 9.
13 O.N.W.A., 1955, s. 8(5); P.O.P.A., 1971, s. 9.

per ton carried, but there has been a vast increase in the oil extracted and transported.

There are misgivings also that legislation of this kind cannot adequately be enforced. Ships' masters and airline pilots report sightings of oil slicks, but it is difficult to identify the offending vessels with sufficient certainty to support a prosecution. New techniques are being developed to compare a sample taken from a slick with one from a suspected vessel, but enforcement against unwilling ship owners and ships' masters will nevertheless remain difficult. The most promising part of the legislation is that which ensures that vessels are properly equipped, and that shore facilities are available for the discharge of oil residues.

The larger oil firms, conscious of their role as polluters, have assisted further by adopting the 'load on top' system, and they claim that this has had considerable effect in containing the total increase in oil spillage. This 'load on top' system replaces an earlier practice of tanker masters which led to so much pollution. Under the earlier system, a tanker returning for a fresh cargo of oil took in sea water as ballast. During the course of its return voyage, it would then wash out its tanks, discharging the resulting mixture of oil and sea water into the sea. Under the 'load on top' system it washes out its tanks but pumps the resulting mixture into a slop tank—either a tank specially built for the purpose or merely one of its tanks designated for that use. In the slop tank the oil and water settle out, so that water only slightly contaminated with oil can be pumped into the sea, leaving behind nearly all the oil washed from the other tanks. At the point of loading the fresh cargo will be taken into all tanks, including the slop tank, where it is loaded on top of the residue of oil which has remained there.

The one difficulty with this system is that the oil in the slop tank is slightly contaminated with sea water. All refineries in this country can deal with this contamination at a cost lower than the price of the oil saved. There is therefore a slight net gain. Unfortunately refineries in some other countries are not so equipped, and therefore do not encourage 'load on top'.

In 1969 an amendment to the 1954 Convention, the effect of which would be to enforce the 'load on top' system, was drawn up and awaits ratification. Other developments are a Conven-

tion on civil liability and another on intervention on the high
seas in cases of oil pollution casualties.

*1969 amendment of the Convention for the Prevention of Pollu-
tion of the Sea by Oil*

As amended the Convention will replace the old prohibitions by
a permitted rate of discharge. Tests have shown that if, while a
ship is under way, oil is discharged at not more than sixty litres
per nautical mile, the deposit has disappeared from view within
two hours, and in temperate waters has been completely oxidised
within twenty-four hours. This rate of discharge has therefore
been adopted as the basis of the Convention.

Ships other than tankers will be permitted to discharge oil
at a rate of not more than sixty litres per sea mile, provdied that
the oil is less than 100 parts per million of the mixture discharged, and the discharge is made as far as practicable from
land.

In the case of tankers, the rate must again not exceed sixty
litres per sea mile, and the total quantity of oil discharged in a
ballast voyage must not exceed 1/15,000 of the total carrying
capacity, and the tanker must be more than fifty miles from
the nearest land.

It is claimed that a ship will be able to work within these
limits, and that this would therefore be a more realistic basis
for legislation. All that would be required would be inspection
of the slop tank at the port of loading to see that 'load on top'
had been used. If it had, there would be no reason why the rate
of sixty litres per mile should have been exceeded or why the
discharge should not have been made well away from land.

To give effect in English law to the provisions of this amendment, the United Kingdom Parliament has already passed the
Oil in Navigable Waters Act, 1971. The provisions of this Act
come into force on such days as the Secretary of State appoints.[14]
Under the Act an offence will be committed if any ship registered in the United Kingdom discharges into any part of the sea

14 O.N.W.A., 1971, s. 12(3). The Oil in Navigable Waters Act, 1971
   (Commencement No. 1) Order, 1971, S.I. 1971 No. 932, brought into
   force from 21 June 1971, sections 2, 3, 5, 7, 8, 9 and 10.

outside the territorial waters of the United Kingdom any crude oil, fuel oil, lubricating oil or heavy diesel oil.[15] When the Act comes into operation, it is anticipated that regulations made under the Oil in Navigable Waters Act, 1955, s. 15, will permit the discharge of sixty litres per mile as agreed in the 1969 amendment.

The special defences provided by the 1955 Act have been slightly tightened by the new Act,[16] and the maximum penalty which may be awarded on summary conviction for unlawful discharges under ss. 1 and 3 of the 1955 Act, and under the Continental Shelf Act, 1964, s. 5, will be increased from £1,000 to £50,000.[17]

Section 8 of the Act gives powers to the Secretary of State enabling him to act when an accident has occurred to or in a ship and there is a danger of oil pollution on a large scale within United Kingdom territorial waters. For the purpose of preventing or reducing oil pollution, or the risk of oil pollution, he will be able to give directions regarding the ship or its cargo to the owner, master, or salvor in possession. If, in the opinion of the Secretary of State, those powers are inadequate, he may himself 'take any action of any kind whatsoever', including taking over control of the ship, or sinking or destroying it.[18] The Act provides rights of compensation if the action was not reasonably necessary, or if the good it did or was likely to do was disproportionately less than the expense incurred.[19]

Civil liability for oil pollution

The task of enforcing civil liability against an owner of a tanker from which our shores are polluted is fraught with difficulty. The act which caused the pollution must have been unlawful, in the sense of giving rise to liability, both in this country and by the law of the flag State. Normally, negligence would have to be proved and the defendant made subject to the jurisdiction of

15 O.N.W.A., 1955, s. 1(2); O.N.W.A., 1971, s. 1.
16 O.N.W.A., 1971, s. 3.
17 O.N.W.A., 1971, s. 7.
18 O.N.W.A., 1971, s. 8(4).
19 O.N.W.A., 1971, schedule 2.

the English course, either by his presence within the jurisdiction, or by seizure of his goods there.[20]

These difficulties can be reduced by international Convention under which the contracting States agree to pass identical legislation on liability, and assist each other with enforcement. To this end the International Convention on Civil Liability for Oil Pollution has been drawn up, but has not yet been ratified by a sufficient number of States to bring it into operation.

Under it, each of the contracting States will by law render the owner of a ship strictly liable for 'pollution damage caused by oil which has escaped or been discharged from the ship'[21] as the result of an occurrence or series of occurrences which have the same origin. He will incur no liability if he can prove that the damage resulted from certain specified causes, namely:

(a) war, hostilities, civil war, insurrection or natural phenomenon of an exceptional, inevitable or irresistible character;[22]
(b) wholly from act or omission by a third party done with intent to cause damage;
(c) negligence or wrongful act of any government or other authority responsible for the maintenance of lights or other navigational aids.

The owner of the vessel will also escape from or reduce his liability if he proves that the damage resulted wholly or partly from the negligence, or act or omission done with intent to cause damage, on the part of the complainant.

No contracting party will be able to claim from the owner otherwise than under the Convention. This is an important restriction, as the Convention limits the liability of the owner to £56 per ton of the ship's tonnage, with a maximum of £5·8 million.[23] The limitation will not apply, however, if the occurrence was the result of the actual fault or privity of the owner.[24]

20 In the *Torrey Canyon* dispute, a sister ship was seized when it entered Hong Kong waters. The claim was settled without resort to the courts.
21 Article III.
22 This last-mentioned cause is equivalent to 'act of God' in English law.
23 These are English equivalents. The Convention figures are 2,000 francs per ton and 210 million francs.
24 Similar words are used in the Carriage of Goods by Sea Act, 1924, Schedule, which may therefore be used as an aid to interpretation of any English legislation. That section, however, adds the words 'or without fault or neglect of agents or servants of the carrier'. See

Owners of vessels, in order to avail themselves of this limit to their liability, will have to establish a fund by deposit or bank guarantee, corresponding to the limit of liability.[25] Claims can then be made against the fund, will be paid if necessary *pro rata*, and any claims by the owner himself for expenses reasonably incurred or sacrifices reasonably made to prevent or minimise pollution damage will rank equally with them.[26] All owners of ships registered in contracting States and carrying more than 2,000 tons of oil as cargo will be required to maintain insurance or other financial security.[27]

The United Kingdom Parliament has now passed the Merchant Shipping (Oil Pollution) Act, 1971, in order to give effect to the Convention. It will be brought into force on days to be appointed by the Secretary of State for Trade and Industry.[27a]

The International Legal Conference of 1969 considered also that a supplementary scheme in the form of an international fund is necessary to ensure that adequate compensation will be available in all cases. It therefore requested the Inter-governmental Maritime Consultative Organisation (I.M.C.O.) to draft a compensation scheme based on an international fund.

Meanwhile the major tanker owners, conscious of their responsibilities, have voluntarily entered into an agreement amongst themselves called the 'Tanker Owners' Voluntary Agreement Concerning Liability for Oil Pollution' (TOVALOP). This is an agreement between tanker owners themselves, and does not go as far in establishing liability as will the 1969 Convention and the legislation passed under it.

The participating tanker owners agree that if, through their negligence, regardless of the degree of fault, a discharge of oil causes damage by pollution to a coastline, or creates grave and imminent danger or damage thereto by pollution, the owner will remove the oil or pay to the government concerned all costs reasonably incurred in its removal, subject to a maximum of $100 per gross registered ton and an overall maximum of $10 million for any one incident.

Hourani *v* Harrison [1927] 32 Com. Cas. 305, where 'or' was held to mean 'and'.
25 Article V(3).
26 Article V(8).
27 Article VII.   27a See Appendix 3.

This liability arises only if the tanker owner or his servants have been negligent, but negligence is presumed. The owner thus escapes liability under the agreement only if he can prove that he was not negligent.

Maximum liability is lower than that under the Convention, and liability depends only on presumed negligence. There is no agreement to be strictly liable. Compensation under the agreement is payable only to governments, but the term is defined to include 'any local government, public authority or organisation within the jurisdiction of such national government on whose behalf such national government shall confirm its readiness and competence to act for the purposes of this agreement'. There is no agreement to compensate individuals. Even governments gain no legal rights under the agreement, since they are not parties to it.[28]

Any payment under the agreement is expressed to be made in full settlement of all claims by the receiving government against the owner, his servants and agents. Therefore when a tanker owner accepts a claim and agrees to pay, that operates and is enforceable in the same way as any settlement of a claim at civil law. There is provision for arbitration.

The tanker owner is also encouraged to clean up his oil spills, irrespective of negligence. He must maintain insurance coverage, and arrangements are made whereby, if he incurred reasonable expenditure in the removal of oil discharged, he will be entitled to insurance indemnity, whether or not he was negligent.

TOVALOP is supplemented by a second voluntary agreement entered into by the major oil companies. This is the 'Contract regarding an Interim Supplement to Tanker Liability for Oil Pollution' (CRISTAL). The only liability of the oil companies under this agreement is to the Oil Companies' Institute for Marine Pollution Ltd. The Institute has constituted a fund to which the oil companies are called upon, and have agreed to, contribute. The function of the Institute under the agreement is to supplement the compensation payable by a party to TOVALOP, if necessary to a maximum of $30 million.

The terms of the agreement provide for an occasion when a

28 The agreement is governed by English law.

party to TOVALOP would have been liable, by the terms of the Convention on Civil Liabilities, 1969, had the agreement been in force, to persons suffering oil pollution damage; or if the Convention has come into force an occasion when the party is liable. If the person sustaining the damage is not fully compensated, the Institute will provide the necessary additional sum subject to a maximum of $30 million.

Whereas TOVALOP provides for compensation to governments and public authorities, CRISTAL is wider in its scope, the undertaking being to compensate all persons who would be entitled under legislation passed in compliance within the Convention. Since the agreement to compensate under CRISTAL is dependent on liability as provided by the 1969 Convention, payment will be made irrespective of negligence, whereas compensation under TOVALOP depends on presumed negligence.

The agreement is governed by the laws of England, and the English courts are given exclusive jurisdiction. It expressly provides that no trust is constituted. The agreement therefore creates no enforceable liabilities to persons suffering pollution damage.

These voluntary agreements were entered into as interim measures pending the imposition of legal liabilities by State legislatures under the Convention.

Convention on Intervention on the High Seas in Cases of Oil Pollution Casualties, 1969

This Convention, if and when ratified by a sufficient number of signatory States, will recognise a right in any government of a State which is a party to take effective action against a ship which, by reason of a marine accident, is threatening to pollute the coast. The State may take such measures on the high seas as may be necessary to prevent, mitigate or eliminate grave and imminent danger to its coastline or related interests from oil pollution. There is an exception in favour of warships or ships on government non-commercial service.

There are provisions for prior consultation with other States, including the flag State, except in cases of extreme emergency. Measures taken must not go beyond what is reasonably necessary, and must be proportionate to the damage, actual or threatened.

Canadian legislation

Canada has expressed dissatisfaction with the Convention on Intervention on the grounds that, although it gives a right to destroy a ship after an accident, it gives no power to take action before the accident has occurred. Moreover, the danger from the presence of oil pollutants in Arctic waters is far greater than in temperate seas. In order to protect the Arctic region near the Canadian mainland and islands. Canada has therefore passed an Arctic Waters Pollution Prevention Act.

This legislation will not directly affect the U.K. but it merits attention on two grounds. It asserts Canadian jurisdiction over a large part of the seas outside Canadian territorial limits. It may well provide a pattern for legislation by other States.

The Act prohibits the deposit of waste of any type in Arctic waters, then empowers the Governor in Council to make regulations prescribing the type and quantity of waste which may be deposited. The Governor in Council may also declare any part of the Arctic waters governed by the Act to be a 'shipping safety control zone' and to make regulations applicable to shipping in that zone, including prohibition on ships of specified classes from navigating in the area. This will enable the Canadian government to prevent tankers of any State from sailing on that part of the high seas.

There is a provision whereby the Governor in Council is empowered to order the destruction of any ship which in Arctic waters is in distress and is likely to deposit waste.

Pollution prevention officers will be appointed who will be empowered to board any ship within a safety control zone, and exercise far-reaching powers, including, with the consent of the Governor in Council, seizing a ship and its cargo.

Escape of oil from sea bed workings or pipelines

By international agreement the United Kingdom has exclusive rights to exploit the natural resources of the sea bed and its subsoil on certain parts of the continental shelf outside its territorial waters. The Continental Shelf Act, 1964, s. 5,[29] seeks to prevent pollution by the escape of oil from sea bed workings or pipelines in these areas. If any crude oil, fuel oil, lubricating or heavy diesel oil escapes into any part of the sea from a pipeline or sea bed working, the owner or operator shall be guilty of an offence. It will be a defence for him to prove that the escape was due to the fact of a person there without his permission, or that neither the escape nor any delay in discovering it was due to want of reasonable care on his part, and that he took all reasonable steps for stopping or reducing it.

Section 1(3) incorporates into the Act ss. 2 and 6 of the Petroleum (Production) Act, 1934. Of the latter Act, s. 2 empowers the Board of Trade to grant licences to search, bore for and get petroleum. Section 6 empowers the Board to make regulations prescribing, *inter alia*, model clauses which shall, unless the Board thinks fit to modify or exclude them, be incorporated in any such licence; and different regulations may be made for different kinds of licence.

The model clauses applicable to licences to drill into the sea bed are found in the Petroleum (Production) Regulations, 1966.[30] Drilling is not to be commenced or abandoned without the written consent of the Minister,[31] and the plugging of a well is to be done in accordance with specifications approved by the Minister. The licensee is to use methods customarily used in good oilfield practice for containing the oil in pipelines or other receptacles,[32] and for all operations so as to prevent the escape of petroleum into surrounding waters.[33] He must comply with instructions given from time to time by the Minister in writing concerning those operations,[34] and they must not interfere unjustifiably with navigation, fishing or the conservation of the living resources of the sea. If there is a breach or non-observance of any of the terms or conditions, the Minister may revoke the licence.[35]

29 As amended by O.N.W.A., 1971, s. 6. See now P.O.P.A., 1971, s. 3.
30 S.I. 1966 No. 898.
31 Clause 13.
32 Clause 15.
33 Clause 16.
34 Clause 17.
35 Clause 33.

8   Solid waste

Common law

At common law a man may deposit waste on his own land, subject to the law of nuisance and the rule in Rylands v Fletcher.[1] The difficulty with the latter is in establishing the dumping as a non-natural use of land. In the case of toxic wastes, however, this should not be difficult.

It has already been noted that common law remedies such as these do little to prevent the growth of pollution. They do not provide the measure of control that society needs.

Statutes

Most of the statutory provisions dealing with the dumping of solid wastes were passed to deal with small accumulations of rubbish. They are to be found in the Public Health Acts and the Civic Amenities Act. There are provisions dealing with industrial alkali waste in the Alkali, etc., Works Regulation Act, 1906, but these have a narrow field of application.

Public Health Acts

The Public Health Act, 1936, empowers local authorities to provide tips for the disposal of the household refuse it collects.[2] The authority may also undertake to collect trade refuse, in which case it must impose charges.[3] There is an exception in the case of inner London, where the authority is under a duty to collect trade refuse.[4] But even where the authority is under a

1 See Section 4, 'Air pollution', under 'Common law'.
2 Section 76.
3 Section 73.
4 London Government Act, 1963, schedule 11, para. 14(1).

duty to collect refuse, and must then necessarily dispose of it, it is liable if the manner of disposal it adopts proves to be a nuisance at law.

In providing tips the authority is subject to planning law, and may have to face objections by local residents at a public enquiry.

The Public Health Acts also give the authorities power to deal with accumulations of waste or rubbish on private land. In any borough or urban district,[5] if it appears to a sanitary inspector that an accumulation of noxious matter ought to be removed, he shall serve a notice on the occupier requiring him to remove it, and if it is not removed within twenty-four hours the inspector may remove it and recover the expenses.[6]

A similar power is given by the Public Health Act, 1961, s. 34. Under this section, if it appears to the local authority that any rubbish on any land in the open air is seriously detrimental to the amenities of the neighbourhood, it may take such steps for removing it as it considers necessary in the interests of amenity. This section does not apply, however, to material collected for, or in the course of, any business.

Civic Amenities Act, 1967

The statutory powers and duties in this Act will doubtless be construed in the light of the general purpose of the Act, which is to protect the amenities of the neighbourhood.

The Act places a duty, not merely a power, on the local authority to remove any motor car abandoned on any land in the open air or on any highway.[7] There is also a power to destroy it.[8] The Act also provides that the person who abandons it shall be guilty of an offence and liable to a fine of up to £100 on the first, and up to £200 on any subsequent conviction. The local authority may recover from him the cost of removal and disposal.[9]

5 The Minister may by order extend this power to any rural district.
6 P.H.A., 1936, s. 79.
7 Section 20.
8 Section 21.
9 Section 23.

Although the authority is duty-bound to remove such vehicles, it is not entitled to do so under this Act if the owner of the land objects, and need not do so if the cost of taking it to the nearest highway is unreasonably high.[10] Section 23 gives similar powers over other things abandoned.

Alkali, etc., Works Regulation Act, 1906

The Act provides that every works in which is used acid or other substance which is capable of liberating sulphuretted hydrogen from alkali waste or the discharge therefrom, shall be carried on in such a manner as not to create a nuisance.[11]

It also provides that alkali waste shall not be deposited or discharged without the best practicable means being used for effectually preventing a nuisance.[12]

Planning control

The deposit of refuse or waste materials on land, notwithstanding that the site has already been used for that purpose, requires planning permission if the superficial area is extended or the height of the deposit is increased and exceeds the level of the land adjoining the site.[13] There is an exception in favour of deposits of industrial waste on a site used for such deposit on 1 July 1948. The result is that any tip existing on that date can be freely increased in extent and height.[14]

Where planning powers exist, carefully drafted conditions can ensure that tipping is restricted to certain classes of waste. A river authority may also be able to exercise some control over both old and new tips. If there is any run-off from a tip into a watercourse, this may be an offence under the Rivers (Prevention of Pollution) Act, 1951, s. 2. For example, a large oil company acquired an old tip and began using it for the deposit of

10 See s. 20 and circular 55/67.
11 Section 3.
12 Section 4.
13 T.C.P.A., 1962, s. 12(3)(b).
14 Under T.C.P.A., 1962, s. 28, the local planning authority can issue a 'discontinuance order' requiring that a particular use of land be discontinued. Compensation must be paid. The power is rarely used.

oily wastes, with resulting pollution of a nearby watercourse. Faced with threats of prosecution by the river authority, the oil company put an end to the practice, and any resumption can be dealt with by a court order under the Rivers (Prevention of Pollution) Act, 1951, s. 3.

The river authorities are not satisfied, however, that their powers are quite adequate. In the first place, they would like an extension of their powers to control discharges to underground strata under the Water Resources Act, 1963, s. 72.[15] In the second place, there is evidence that the maximum punishments and the punishments actually awarded are too low. An order under s. 3 is not an appropriate method of dealing with occasional or illegal tipping such as is sometimes done by drivers of commercial disposal firms. The maximum fine on summary conviction is £100, and those imposed are frequently well below this. Under the Salmon and Freshwater Fisheries Act, 1923, the maximum fine is a mere £50, with £5 per day for a continuing offence.

In a case brought by Yorkshire Ouse and Hull River Authority in 1968 a driver was seen discharging concentrated black acidic sludge over the shoulder of a tip. The tip was used by the local rural district council, and at the time the entrance was barred and locked. The driver was employed by a commercial waste disposal company. The fumes from the discharge were such that an approach to the tanker tap to stop the discharge required protective gloves. The sludge ran onto scrubland that sloped downwards to a watercourse. The driver admitted discharging similar loads at that point twice in the previous seven days, but claimed that he had the permission of the tip attendant. There was some conflict of evidence on the latter point. The banks of the watercourse were for about half a mile below the tip coated with black sludge which burned the skin on contact. The defendent company arranged to remove as much waste sludge as possible from the tip, and fully co-operated in cleaning the banks and bed of the watercourse. As trout had been killed by the discharge it was prosecuted under the Salmon and Freshwater Fisheries Act, 1923, s. 8. It pleaded guilty and was fined £10.

In other cases fines of the order of £20 and £50 have been

15 See p. 23 *supra.*

imposed. Although convictions such as these do not necessarily mean that there has been wilful misconduct by the defendant companies, it is doubtful whether fines as low as these put sufficient pressure on them to tighten their control. On the other hand, in fairness to those companies, it might be appropriate to introduce the type of special defence available under the Trade Descriptions Act, 1968, s. 23. Under such a provision it would be a defence to prove that the commission of the offence was due to the act or default of another person, or an accident or some other cause beyond his control, and that the accused took all reasonable precautions and exercised all due diligence to avoid the commission of the offence by himself or any person under his control.[16]

If the recommendations of the Key committee[17] are put into effect, tips and disposal firms will be brought under local government control. The larger local authorities will then authorise disposals of industrial wastes, solid and liquid, and can ensure that the best methods and techniques of disposal are used. It remains to be seen just what these powers will be, and how they are used. They could be extensive enough to ensure that valuable tipping space is put to the best use. Where, for example, there is a dry mining shaft which goes down below the level of the water table, this should clearly be used for toxic wastes. At present it may be privately owned and filled with inert matter, leaving a difficult local problem for those seeking to dispose of highly toxic wastes.

Whatever powers are given to local authorities, the legal rights and the interests of people living nearby will still need protection. The retention of common law remedies will protect their legal rights,[18] while the planning procedure, under which an application to tip must be publicised and open to objection, will protect other interests.

There has been a voluntary move by the National Coal Board, which has indicated that it is prepared to discuss with a planning

16 As to the interpretation of this section see Tesco Supermarkets v Nattrass [1971] 2 All E.R. 127.
17 Ministry of Housing and Local Government, *Report of the Technical Committee on the Disposal of Toxic Solid Wastes*, H.M.S.O., London, 1970.
18 See p. 98.

authority at area level any minor works for improving the appearance of colliery spoil heaps. The Forestry Commission has said has it will be glad to give advice on the planting of trees, and the regional controller of the Ministry of Agriculture, Fisheries and Food will give advice on planting grass.[19]

The Litter Act, 1958

The Litter Act, 1958, makes it an offence to drop or deposit and leave in any place in the open air to which the public are entitled or permitted to have access without payment, anything so as to cause defacement by litter. A fine of up to £100 may be imposed.[20]

The Act is not enforced, and it is very doubtful if it is generally enforceable. Nonetheless it has been supplemented by the Dangerous Litter Act, 1971, which increases the maximum penalty and provides that in sentencing the court shall have regard not only to defacement of open spaces, but also to the nature of the litter and and resulting risk to persons or animals or damage to property.

The law relating to the dumping of wastes is very patchy. There seem to be adequate provisions for dealing with small quantities of rubbish and things abandoned, but there is some misgiving about how these powers are used in practice.

Sections 3 and 4 of the Alkali Act deal specifically with industrial waste, but are too narrow in two respects. They apply only to a small class of waste products, and they require only that no nuisance shall be created. This means that there shall be no such interference with others as would at law justify an action or prosecution for nuisance. Any legislation dealing with the deposit of waste products should surely concern itself not only with nuisance but also with public health and amenity.

19 See circular 26/59.
20 Dangerous Litter Act, 1971, s. 1.

9   Schemes of voluntary restraint

Pesticides

There is little legislation governing the distribution and use of pesticides. Under the Town and Garden Chemicals Act, 1967, the Minister may make regulations imposing requirements as to the labelling and marketing of pesticides and herbicides. The Agriculture (Poisonous Substances) Act, 1952, protects employees against the risks of poisoning. The safety precautions which protect farmer, worker and the general public are provided by the Pesticides Safety Precautions Scheme.[1]

This is a voluntary scheme agreed between government departments and the pesticide industry. Under it, distributors—which includes manufacturers and importers—undertake

1. To notify new pesticides or new use of existing pesticides to the Ministry of Agriculture, the Ministry of Health and the corresponding Scottish departments.
2. To ascertain and disclose to the same government departments all information needed to enable them to advise on the precautionary measures which should be employed when products containing those pesticides are used.
3. Not to introduce such products until agreement has been reached on the appropriate precautionary measures.
4. To include the agreed precautions and common name of the active ingredient on the label of every container.
5. To withdraw the product from the market if recommended to do so by the government departments.

An advisory committee and scientific sub-committee consider whether the use of the substance will involve risk to the user, the consumer of the treated crop, or wildlife. If they are satisfied, the substance can then be cleared for safety. Clearance may be:

1   There is a similar Veterinary Products Safety Precautions Scheme.

(a) trials clearance, (b) limited clearance, (c) provisional commercial clearance, (d) commercial clearance. There are provisions for subsequent review if evidence reveals a risk which was not previously studied. On clearance, guidance is given on markings and instructions for use, standard phrases being used.

This method of giving clearance is adopted because many of the active substances are new products whose effects are not fully understood. The persons with the greatest knowledge of them are those who did the experimental work leading to the production of the substance. Ministry scientific advisers merely satisfy themselves that an adequate programme of tests has been followed. As experience grows, the programme is extended to cover risks which were not previously appreciated or adequately covered.

In addition to the markings and instructions which accompany the product when sold, there are standard codes of practice for ground and air spraying. Although it is possible that members of the public may be sprayed, when the pesticide has been diluted for use there is a safety factor of usually 100. Dangers arise from misuse of the undiluted product. There is a danger from farm workers handling it carelessly, and a danger from residues which may be left in the tins.

It is this latter danger which has given rise to the only fatal accident. A can not completely emptied found its way to a scrap merchant's yard in Ipswich. A youth flattening the tins was splashed by the residue and died. Instructions on the tins now emphasise that they must be emptied completely into the tank where it is being diluted for use. Consideration has been given to making all containers returnable, but owing to difficulty in working such a scheme, and the fact that there is only one reported fatal accident in about twenty years, the idea has been rejected.

Non-fatal accidents and diseases in agriculture[2]

	Chemicals and poisons	All causes
1963–64	19	11,866
1964–65	27	10,408
1965–66	12	9,514

2 Ministry of Agriculture, *Report on Safety, Health, Welfare and Wages in Agriculture, 1 October 1966–31 December 1967*, H.M.S.O., London, 1968.

There have been a number of non-fatal accidents amongst farm workers, but these are a very small proportion of accidents from all causes, as can be seen from the preceding table.

Figures for later years are given on a different basis, but show similarly low proportions.

All commercial producers and distributors have accepted the scheme. The only persons who by-pass it are farmers who may import small quantities for their own use and perhaps to sell to neighbours. Even here the substances imported will almost certainly have been subjected to similar, but compulsory, approval schemes in the country of origin. Since the inception of the voluntary scheme there have been only two evasions by U.K. distributors.

The effect of pesticides on the environment is kept under continuous review. In particular, a Research Committee on Toxic Chemicals has been established by the Agricultural Research Council. Its terms of reference are:

1. To keep under review research done under the auspices of the Research Councils on the effect of toxic chemicals used in agriculture and food storage; and to make recommendations for future research.
2. To review the research in progress or required to ensure the safe use of any toxic chemical (including any potentially toxic chemicals on sale to farmers for veterinary surgeons, but excluding toxic effects on the animals being treated) specifically referred to the committee by the Advisory Committee on Pesticides and other Toxic Chemicals; or to advise on measures needed to make such a review.
3. To make periodic reports to the Agricultural Research Council and, through it, to the other Research Councils and to the Ministers concerned.

The Advisory Committee on Pesticides and other Toxic Chemicals referred to was established by the Department of Education and Science, and reported in 1964 and 1969 on the effects of certain persistent organochloride pesticides.[3]

Despite the claims by both government and the industry that the voluntary precautions scheme is a success, and despite the

3 *Review of Certain Persistent Organochloride Pesticides used in Great Britain*, H.M.S.O., London, 1964, and *Further Review of Certain Persistent Organochloride Pesticides used in Great Britain*, H.M.S.O., London, 1969.

fact that these claims seem to be justified, legislation has been drafted to replace it with a similar but compulsory scheme. There is doubt whether this legislation will serve any useful purpose. The present scheme works smoothly and reasonably quickly. Speed is important to the British firms, who face keen competition from abroad. About £1 million is spent on developing a new product: a delay of a few months in marketing it could be costly. There are fears that a compulsory scheme would work more slowly. These fears are not necessarily well founded, but there is perhaps another and greater danger. Whereas while the scheme is voluntary everyone from producer to farmer has usually nothing to fear from frank disclosure, if it becomes compulsory and backed by criminal penalties, attitudes may well change. As long as both sides are satisfied with the present system, and as long as the safety record remains good, there seems little point in introducing legislation, with its necessary enforcement measures of inspections, prosecutions and penalties.

Although the record is good, danger to the public remains. Producers recognise this by covering the risk by insurance policies. There seems to be a case here for imposing strict liability on the producer. In parallel cases this has been done.

Normally a person is not liable in tort for damage caused by his acts in producing, selling or using things unless negligence is proved. In some exceptional cases, however, liability without proof of negligence is imposed. If I, for my own purposes, bring onto my land something which might do damage if it escapes, and if this is a 'special use bringing with it increased dangers',[4] I am liable at common law for damage consequent on the escape, even though there may have been no negligence on my part.[5] Again, the legislators have recognised that operators of nuclear installations create unusual and increased dangers, and likewise have imposed strict liability on them.[6] They have even gone further in this case and provided that no liability shall fall upon any other persons if damage is done by a nuclear incident.[6]

In the case of pesticides, it is admitted by the producers that even though all care is taken in production and testing, an

4   Rickards *v* Lothian [1913] A.C. 263 at 280.
5   Rule in Rylands *v* Fletcher. See pp. 56–7 *supra*.
6   See p. 72 *supra*.

area of uncertainty and danger still remains. Knowing this, for their own purposes they launch the product on to the market. It creates unusual and special dangers for both users and the public. If the consumer, normally a farmer, has used the product strictly according to the manufacturer's or distributor's instructions, and unexpected damage is done, this seems to be similar in principle to the rule in Rylands v Fletcher, which imposes strict liability. It would be almost impossible to establish negligence on the part of any manufacturer who had complied with the requirements of the voluntary scheme. Yet, despite the precautions taken under the scheme, there remains an area of doubt when the substance is launched on to the market. Since the manufacturer knowingly creates such a risk, it is submitted that liability should fall on him.

Detergents

The widespread use of detergents in place of soap led to difficulties at sewage works and to pollution of inland watercourses. Most of the early detergents were 'hard', that is, non-biodegradable; and, besides passing through the biological processes of sewage works, in the early 1950s rendered them 25 per cent less efficient. Once in the watercourses they could affect water supplies, and in some cases caused foaming, which was a considerable nuisance. This foaming can be reduced by measures taken by the river authorities, but the solution clearly lay in the production of 'soft' detergents.

In 1957 a Standing Technical Committee in Synthetic Detergents was appointed by the Minister of Housing and Local Government, with the following terms of reference: 'To keep under review the difficulties, or risks of difficulty, arising in sewage works, rivers and water supply as a result of the use of synthetic detergents.' The committee includes representatives of the Department of the Environment, Ministry of Agriculture, Fisheries and Food, the Scottish Office, the Laboratory of the Government Chemist, representatives from local authorities and river authorities, and representatives of manufacturers nominated by the C.B.I. It has published reports annually.

No statutory controls have been imposed, but the manufacturers have undertaken not to sell for domestic use from 1 January 1964 any hard anionic detergents. This form of voluntary restraint has proved workable mainly because a few large manufacturers dominate the market. They have developed new detergents which, although at first more expensive to produce, can now be made more cheaply. There have been only two known breaches of the undertaking. Supervision is by the industry, with reports sent to the Standing Technical Committee, the C.B.I. and the particular firm concerned.

Even this restricted undertaking has resulted in a marked improvement in rivers.[7] One advantage of the voluntary scheme is that firms are willing to report breaches of the agreement, whereas they might not do so if they thought a criminal prosecution would follow. Furthermore the scheme is flexible; no fixed standard is laid down. Unfortunately this is necessary, for although 'softness' has increased, so over the years has the quantity of detergent used, rendering further improvement essential to the mere maintenance of standards of river water. There is therefore a continuing pressure for improvement. In Western Germany 80 per cent biodegradability is obligatory: in the U.K. new sewage works now extract 90 per cent, and in some cases 95 per cent.

The scheme is regarded as meeting the requirements of the European agreement on detergents of 1968, to which the U.K. is a party.[8]

The committee is now working towards an agreement on detergents, produced for industrial use.

Sea dumping

An enormous quantity of waste matter is dumped in the sea beyond the three-mile limit each year.[9] The tendency to use the

7 T. Waldemeyer, 'Analytical records of synthetic detergent concentrations', a paper presented at the Institute of Water Pollution Control, Metropolitan and Southern Branch meeting, November 1970.
8 *European Agreement on the Restriction on the Use of Certain Detergents in Washing and Cleaning Products*, E.T.S. No. 64, October 1968, Council of Europe, Strasbourg, 1968.
9 For details of the nature and quantities of the substances see 'Questionnaire on the Pollution of the Marine Environment', I.M.C.O., 1969.

sea for dumping has increased in recent years, particularly with the tightening of controls inland.

There are no legal restrictions on dumping beyond the three-mile limit, except those on the discharge of oil, but there is a voluntary scheme for controlled dumping administered by the Ministry of Agriculture, Fisheries and Food. Under this scheme a person intending to dump informs the Ministry of the nature, source and quantity of the substance. A sample may be requested for analysis, but there is no compulsion. Normally the applicant under the scheme suggests the site where he is to drop the waste. These proposals are checked by scientists at the Ministry's Fisheries Laboratory at Burnham on Crouch, and formal approval is given by the Ministry.

When the waste has been dropped, a return is sent to the Ministry. The information in the returns may be checked against the ship's log, but no other check is made, nor any form of supervision maintained. There is no monitoring of the designated sea areas, merely general monitoring round the coast and routine tests of fish and shellfish. Most of the dumping is by commercial disposal firms.

The government is aware of the growing seriousness of the problem of sea dumping, and is reviewing the need for greater national and international control.[10]

10 See Hansard, 4 November 1970.

10 Some general observations

It has become clear from the foregoing that there is a dichotomy in English law relating to pollution control. On the one hand the common law gives the individual certain rights, which may be asserted by an action in the courts taken at his own instance. If he establishes his claim he is entitled to compensation for the damage he has suffered and can ask for an injunction to restrain the polluter, which the court may grant at its discretion. As we have seen, the emissions permitted at common law vary according to the rights protected and the form of action taken. A riparian owner or anyone deriving rights from him can sue for any degree of impurity; so can one who founds his action in trespass or Rylands v Fletcher, where such actions are applicable. But if the action is in nuisance for interference with personal comfort or enjoyment, the standards applied are not absolute, but relative to the quality of the environment already found in that neighbourhood generally.

On the other hand, a number of public authorities exercise a variety of statutory powers of pollution control, which aim to achieve a clean environment for the benefit of the public or sections of the public, but often lay down standards which run parallel to yet are different from those required at common law. Many river authority consents permit a degree of pollution which is sufficient to give any riparian owner a right of action in the civil courts. Conversely, a local authority will often enforce standards under the Clean Air Acts which in many districts are substantially higher than those demanded at common law. These statutory powers of control are normally backed by criminal sanctions, but in no case is the individual allowed a right of objection to a proposed discharge, and in no case has he a right of action for breach of statutory duty[1] against the person who

---

1 See pp. 9–10 *supra*.

exceeds the permitted rate.[2]

The result is two completely unrelated systems, which operate according to different criteria. If our law is to serve the two functions of ensuring acceptable standards of environmental quality, and compensating those who suffer damage where pollution occurs, and if it is to do so with the consistency that justice naturally demands, these two systems must at least be based on one coherent theory of man's legal rights and duties towards those who share his environment.

A first step would be to rid ourselves of the old rule that what amounts to a nuisance must be judged according to the existing character of the neighbourhood in which it occurs.[3] In 1879 Thesiger L.J. said, 'What would be a nuisance in Belgrave Square would not necessarily be so in Bermondsey.'[4] In modern terms this means that the resident in Bermondsey is not entitled in law to the same environmental quality as the resident in Belgrave Square. At the United Nations Conference on the Human Environment to be held in Stockholm in 1972, it is likely that there will be a declaration of man's right to a clean environment. It is doubtful if even an Englishman would dare to proffer Thesiger's dictum as a contribution. Yet it remains law in England today. The rule has permitted slow deterioration of the environment in some areas, lower standards are accepted, whereas today we are seeking improvement: and it admits of social inequality which might have been accepted in 1879 but which is not accepted today, at least in terms of environmental quality.

The second and greater step would be to marry the two systems of public control and private rights. This could not be done, however, without a radical change in our present system of control as at present administered, and without some loss of right by individuals.

Apart from the few provisions under which standards are fixed, such as the Clean Air Acts and Oil on Navigable Waters Acts, most of our systems are flexible, giving public authorities

2 The only comparable rights are: public nuisance (see p. 55 *supra*), action for breach of statutory duty to provide wholesome water taken against a statutory water undertaker (see p. 42 *supra*).
3 See p. 55 *supra*.
4 Sturgess *v* Bridgman (1879) 11 Ch.D. 856.

wide areas of discretion. River authorities exercise a discretion in granting consents; alkali inspectors have some discretion in what they will require as provisional best practicable means; many sea fishery committees have bye-laws which leave them areas of discretion; the Secretary of State for Trade and Industry will have a discretion in issuing notices under the Civil Aviation Act, 1971. In exercising these discretions the authorities concerned attempt to balance the interests of those members of the public who stand to be affected by pollution against the interests of the industry, remembering that a viable industry is a matter of public interest also.

The authorities frequently go further. They often refrain from prosecuting, even in the face of repeated breaches, if they are convinced that the polluter is taking reasonable steps to remedy the breach, and that prosecution will serve no useful purpose. This form of restraint can be exercised because the authority is often the only person empowered to bring a prosecution. Both local authorities and industrial firms frequently exceed consent conditions, the river authority taking the view that notice that improvement is required, advice and warning are often more effective to achieve a permanent improvement than immediate prosecution.

To combine civil remedies with these forms of control, so that the same standards applied in both civil and criminal law, would involve two radical changes. Some of the measures of discretion would be taken from the public authorities, and there would be some reduction in the rights or remedies of individuals.

The public authorities' discretion would be reduced because any person affected by a discharge would have a right of action whenever a breach of the control provisions occurred. This would not necessarily happen frequently, for an excess discharge into an already polluted river may make no real difference, and the damage effect of an excess discharge to the atmosphere may not be traceable to its source. In some cases, however, it could have the salutary effect of ensuring that realistic standards were set.

There would in many cases be a loss of individual rights if the common law and statutory standards were to become one. Obviously the common law standard of water purity could not immediately be enforced without disastrous results to industry. In practice, when the two standards exist side by side, river authority controls today set the effective standards. Not for a long time, if ever, could absolute freedom from pollution be enforced. If, therefore, it was enacted that consents granted by a river authority established the standards which would be enforceable at civil law, this would mean that individuals would lose their rights to unpolluted water. Where consents took away a man's rights to compensation, that would be a confiscation of his rights. Where they merely prevented him from obtaining an injunction, it would mean compulsory purchase of his rights.

Compulsory purchase is unpleasant, but may often be justified. Few would suggest that a large steelworks should be closed merely because of an unpleasant smell or because of fumes from coke ovens or converters, or merely because the trees in the neighbourhood were not healthy. But whenever Parliament has given powers of compulsory purchase it has always given also a right of objection. As we have already noted in the section on inland waters, non-disclosure of proposals to discharge into rivers makes objection impossible, and in practice similar information given to alkali inspectors and sea fishery committees is treated as confidential. As long as this information remains so, no right to object can be given. In practice an alkali inspector, a river authority and any other public authority exercising control always takes account of representations made to it by interested persons, but these representations can be made only after the discharge has started, and often without any detailed knowledge of what is being discharged. As we have noted,[5] in the majority of cases this confidentiality is not necessary to protect the private interests of the discharger, and with disclosure better protection can be given to other private individuals and to the public generally. Similar disclosures are made at planning enquiries: there are good reasons for requiring disclosure on other occasions, with a right to apply for non-disclosure where special circumstances justify it.

Once facts or proposals are known, there can be a right of objection by interested persons, with rights of appeal similar to

5   See p. 35 *supra*.

those now enjoyed by the ones who discharge the wastes. Facts thus disclosed could also be used in a civil action for compensation. Of course, disclosure of exactly what a factory is discharging into a river is 'handing an action on a plate' to riparian owners downstream, but any change which ensures that due compensation is paid can hardly be a ground for objection.

There is now pressure for recognition of rights in all individuals to standards of cleanliness in their environment. Any decision to grant recognition to such rights will be a political decision to be made by the legislature. Whatever form it may take, it will necessarily involve less freedom for public authorities in the exercise of their powers of control, and a far greater degree of disclosure by those who seek to discharge their waste into the environment.

Liability for accidental discharges

If an accident causes pollution, the common law rule of negligence usually applies. A person is liable in law for the foreseeable consequences of his negligence, but entitled to a contribution from any other person whose negligence was a contributary cause. Negligence must be established by the plaintiff, therefore in the absence of evidence his claim will usually fail. In some circumstances, however, the court will accept that the event could not have occurred without the defendant's negligence, as when he is in sole control of an ordinary operation without interference from any other person. The facts then speak for themselves to raise a presumption of negligence. In the absence of any further evidence the plaintiff will then succeed.

In one class of case the common law imposes liability even when there has been no negligence—those cases to which the rule in Rylands v Fletcher applies. The rule is explained briefly on pp. 56–7 *supra* but in this context merits closer examination. In the leading case[6] Lord Blackburn expressed it in the following terms:

the person who for his own purposes brings onto his land and col-

6 Rylands *v* Fletcher (1866) L.R. 1 Ex. 268 at 279–80.

lects and keeps there anything likely to do mischief if it escapes, must keep it in at his peril, and, if he does not do so, is *prima facie* answerable for all the damage which is the natural consequence of its escape.

The application of this rule of strict liability has been limited to what is called, 'non-natural user'. This restriction was explained in the judgement of the Privy Council in Rickards *v* Lothian:[7]

It must be some special use, bringing with it increased danger to others, and must not be the ordinary use of the land or such use as is proper for the general benefit of the community.

The phrase 'proper for the general benefit of the community' is restrictive. In Read *v* Lyons[8] the House of Lords doubted whether this rule applied to the running of a munitions factory in time of war. Nevertheless it has been held that the storage of water and gas in bulk comes within the rule.

The courts have tended to restrict the application of the rule in Rylands *v* Fletcher, but Parliament has shown itself more ready to impose strict liability. The issue is very relevant to pollution cases. If one accepts the broad principle that anyone who, for his own purposes, collects a substance which, by reason of its bulk or its nature, can cause exceptional dangers if it escapes from control should be strictly liable for any escape and subsequent damage, then one must accept strict liability for certain forms of pollution.

It might be argued that the transport of oil and the use of pesticides are 'for the general benefit of the community'. No doubt the community does benefit, but the use of 'super-tankers' which lack manoeuvrability in close waters brings additional and unusual hazards, and certain types of pesticide bring unusual and sometimes unknown dangers. Moreover the benefits are not necessarily enjoyed to the same extent by all. It seems equitable that those who create the unusual risks should be strictly liable in the first place, but able to pass the resulting costs as well as the benefits to their consumers.

Parliament has imposed the strictest form of liability in the Nuclear Installations Act, 1965. This Act not only provides that

7 [1913] A.C. 263 at 280.
8 [1947] A.C. 156.

the nuclear operator shall be strictly liable, but shall remain so for nuclear matter which has left his hands until, broadly speaking, it has become the responsibility of another operator.[9] Furthermore, if an operator is liable for injury or damage resulting from a nuclear incident, all other persons are absolved from liability.

Such strictness may be justified in the case of nuclear substances, for few people other than the operators have knowledge of how they should be handled. In the cases of other seriously polluting substances such as bulk oil and pesticides, there seems no reason why the person from whose control the substance escaped to do damage should not be strictly liable in the first place, but also no reason why in some circumstances other people involved should not in turn be liable to contribute because of their negligence.[10]

There are other grounds for imposing strict liability on operators, and even for relieving other persons from liability for their own negligence. Tanker owners can estimate the rate at which accidents to their vessels will occur. Although any individual accident may not be foreseeable, they can foresee that a certain number will happen each year. By putting their tankers to sea they have created a situation which carries known dangers, and consequences which can be foreseen and estimated. If everyday life is to be made hazardous by such traffic, there is good reason why those who benefit from the traffic should pay for these foreseeable consequences. (The principle has obvious application to road traffic accidents. It has long been suggested that persons injured should be compensated, irrespective of negligence, from a common fund maintained by a charge on all road users.) The tanker owners as initiators and first beneficiaries should then carry primary liability, but of course they will pass a due share of the burden to the consumers.[10]

Manufacturers and distributors of pesticides belong to another category to whom the broad principle underlying the rule in Rylands *v* Fletcher may be applied. Any person who, for his own benefit, puts on to the market a substance, and who knows

9   See N.I.A., 1965, s. 7.
10 Under the Merchant Shipping (Oil Pollution) Act, strict liability is imposed on owners of marine oil tankers. See Appendix 3.

from experience that it belongs to a class which may carry unknown dangers, should be strictly liable for damage which it causes when used according to his instructions. Under the Pesticides Precautions Scheme the manufacturer must carry out certain tests, and would almost certainly be absolved of negligence, yet he knows that there is still some element of doubt. For the benefit of himself and his customers he launches the product. On principle these beneficiaries should be liable for any damage to other members of the public.

Planning

A review of legal and administrative controls over pollution is not complete without an examination of the role of planning authorities, but this is a subject large enough to be treated separately in another volume in this series. It is therefore sufficient here to indicate the place of planning in the general system, if we may call it that, of pollution control.

Much can be done by good planning to prevent or reduce the ill effects of pollution. Sources of noise can be moved away from centres of population or can be shielded[11] from people. Factories can be sited where the effect of discharges to water will be minimised[12] or where because of meteorological conditions their discharges to air will be dispersed rather than concentrated. With careful planning, the natural resources of an area can be used to best effect. A good example of this is seen in Western Germany, where of two parallel rivers the Ruhr is used to carry away discharges whilst the Emscher is retained for water supply. In the United Kingdom rivers of high amenity value and which bear game fish are usually carefully protected by planning authorities and river authorities, while industry is often concentrated near rivers already highly polluted.

Unfortunately, the pattern of our local planning areas does not permit this form of control to be used to the best effect. There is in many parts of the country a maze of small areas, and

11 See p. 84 *supra*.
12 The much criticised planning decision to permit the building of a brewery at Samlesbury was made principally because a new sewage works nearby could deal effectively with the discharges.

—to make a sensible distribution of development less likely—
many of the authorities are anxious to attract development
within their own boundaries. A better control of the environment could be achieved if planning were on a regional scale.
The planning authority would then be more able to permit or
attract industrial development but to site it so as to minimise
the effect on the environment. So long as industry produces
polluting wastes this form of planning will be needed if we are
to accommodate it with the least damage or interference and to
make the best use of natural resources.

Larger planning authorities would also make possible a
closer and more effective co-ordination of the work of the
various pollution control authorities of the area. Good planning
can make the work of river authorities, alkali inspectors and
public health officers easier, and good planning necessarily
entails close co-operation with them. In Lancashire alone there
are at present eighteen local planning authorities, not counting
those exercising delegated powers, only two river authorities
and alkali inspectorate districts. None of their boundaries
coincides. Co-ordination between the planning and development and control of river pollution would obviously be easier
and more effective with fewer and larger planning authorities.

The proposed reorganisation of local government will help.[13]
Under the proposals as they stand at present, the geographical
area of Lancashire will then be covered almost entirely by three
authorities exercising broad planning powers. Although this
will be far from an ideal solution, it will provide an administrative framework within which planning and pollution control
authorities can work together more effectively. The new approach to planning developed since the passing of the Town
and Country Planning Act, 1968, under which local planning
authorities co-operate more closely with Regional Economic
Planning Councils and, where appropriate, with adjacent planning authorities to produce 'structure plans', combined with the

13 The government proposals for reorganisation make it clear that land-
use planning will be increasingly dependent on regional strategies,
and their broad planning policies and the development of both
structure and local plans will rest with county councils. See *Local
Government in England: Government Proposals for Reorganisation*,
Cmnd. 4584, H.M.S.O., London, 1971, paras. 11 and 21.

greater awareness of the effects of polluting discharges, give reason to hope that in the future the broad lines of development will be drawn in such a way that damage to property, natural resources and amenity can be kept to an acceptable minimum, and where it cannot be eliminated can at least be localised.

Appendix 1 Construction and Use Regulations, 1969 Schedule 10

Conditions mentioned in regulation 89(2)

1. At the time when the noise emitted by the vehicle is measured, the microphone of the apparatus shall be so placed that the top of the microphone is set at a height of not less than 3 feet 9 inches and not more than 4 feet 1 inch above a point at ground level which is not less than 17 feet away from the nearest part of the carriageway on which the vehicle is being used.

2.—(1) For the purposes of this paragraph, the area in the vicinity of the microphone shall be treated as comprising areas the situation and extent of which shall be determined by reference to a line joining a point at ground level above which the microphone is placed to the said nearest part of the carriageway and in accordance with the diagram at the end of this Schedule including the directions contained therein; and the said areas shown marked I, II, III or IV on the said diagram are hereafter in this Schedule respectively referred to as the areas so marked.

(2) At the time when the noise is measured there shall not be:

   (a) in the area marked I, any physical object higher than 2 feet above ground level;
   (b) in the area marked II, any physical object higher than 3 feet above ground level; and
   (c) in the areas marked III or IV, any physical object higher than 5 feet above ground level:

Provided that the requirements at (c) above shall not apply in relation to the following objects or to any of them, that is to say:

   (i) to plants, shrubs, trees or any other kind of vegetation, or
   (ii) to any physical object, of which a continuous surface less than 1 foot wide over all its height would be visible in daylight, to a person looking at it from the point above which the microphone is placed and whose eye level is at the height of the microphone.

(3) For the purpose of sub-paragraph (2) of this paragraph, neither the vehicle nor any part thereof, nor any person nor thing in or on the vehicle, nor the apparatus nor any part thereof, nor any persons being less than 3 in number attending the apparatus, shall be taken into account.

3. At the time when the noise emitted by the vehicle is measured, the vehicle shall be wholly or partly on a part of the road which falls within the area marked IV on the said diagram.

4. As soon as the vehicle has left the area marked IV on the said diagram the apparatus shall be used to measure the sound level (A weighting) in decibels of such noise as is then capable of affecting the sound level indications of the apparatus, such measurement being carried out in the manner in which the measurement of the sound emitted by the vehicle was carried out and under the conditions applicable under the foregoing provisions of this Schedule, excluding paragraphs 2(2)(*c*) and 3.

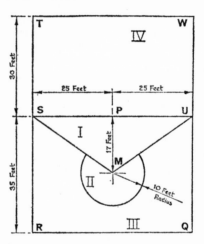

Diagram directions (*including key and dimensions*)

M   a point at ground level above which the microphone is placed.
P   the nearest part of the carriageway to the microphone.
The area marked I consists of the triangle MSU.
The area marked II consists of so much of the circle of radius 10 feet with centre at M as does not enclose any part of the area marked I.
The area marked III consists of so much of the rectangle RSUQ as does not enclose any parts of the areas marked I or II.
The area marked IV consists of the rectangle STWU.

Dimensions

The distance MP is not less than 17 feet.
The lengths of SR and UQ are each 35 feet.
The lengths of TW, SU, and RQ are each 50 feet.
The lengths of SP and PU are each 25 feet.
The lengths of TS and WU are each 30 feet.

Appendix 2 Prosecutions and convictions for offences relating to pollution

Prosecutions and convictions in 1968 for offences relating to pollution*

Act under which proceedings taken	Number of persons proceeded against	Charge withdrawn or dismissed	Persons found guilty			Otherwise disposed of
			Total	Fined	Otherwise dealt with	
Alkali, etc, Works Regulation Act, 1906:						
in England	1	–	1	1	–	–
in Scotland	nil	–	–	–	–	–
Clean Air Acts, 1956 and 1968:						
in England	112	8	103	93	10	1
in Scotland	161	4	157	134	23	–
Regulations 24, 25, 26, 84 and 85 of the Motor Vehicles (Construction and Use) Regulations, 1969	2,672	68	2,582	2,510	72	22
Rivers (Prevention of Pollution) Acts, 1951 and 1961	33	6	25	23	2	2
Rivers (Prevention of Pollution) (Scotland) Acts, 1951 and 1965	3	–	3	3	–	–
Oil in Navigable Waters Act, 1955, s. 3:						
prosecutions by Board of Trade†	nil	–	–	–	–	–
prosecutions by Harbour Authorities	64	2	62	62‡	–	–
Radioactive Substances Act, 1960:						
in England	1	–	1	1	–	–
in Scotland and Wales	nil	–	–	–	–	–

* Information given in reply to a Parliamentary question. See Hansard, 15 April 1970.
† During 1969 the Board of Trade brought summary proceedings against two vessels for discharging oil into the territorial sea. The masters were fined £150 and £500 respectively.
‡ Of these, thirty-four were fined less than £100, nine from £100 to £199, ten from £200 to £299, and nine £300 or over, including one fine of the £1,000 maximum.
N.B. This table is complete for the provisions shown. Information on prosecutions and convictions for other offences relating to pollution is not available.

Persons prosecuted and those found guilty in 1968 for certain
non-motoring offences relating to pollution in England and Wales

Act under which proceedings taken	Number of persons pro-ceeded against	Charge withdrawn or dismissed	Persons found guilty			Other-wise disposed of
			Total	Fined	Other-wise dealt with	
Noise Abatement Act, 1960 (whole Act)	657	13	640	639	1	4
Water Resources Act, 1963 (whole Act)*	11	1	10	10	–	–
Section 19, Civic Amenities Act, 1967*	557	34	520	512	8	3

Orders for dealing with nuisances
(nuisances by noise cannot be
distinguished from other
nuisances)*

Year	Applications	Orders made
1968	1578	719
1969	1337	721

* These do not necessarily all relate to pollution offences within the definition
given on page 1.

Persons prosecuted and those found guilty in 1969 for certain
non-motoring offences relating to pollution in England and Wales

Act under which proceedings taken	Number of persons pro-ceeded against	Charge withdrawn or dismissed	Persons found guilty			Other-wise disposed of
			Total	Fined	Other-wise dealt with	
Noise Abatement Act, 1960 (whole Act)	466	14	450	440	10	2
Water Resources Act, 1963 (whole Act)*	16	3	12	11	1	1
Section 19, Civic Amenities Act 1967*	730	44	680	667	13	6
1970						
Section 19, Civic Amenities Act 1967	778	22	752	733	19	4

* These do not necessarily all relate to pollution offences within the definition given on page 1.

Prosecutions and findings of guilt in 1968 for certain motoring offences relating to noise or pollution in England and Wales

(1) Offence	(2) Offences dealt with by prosecution	(3) Charges withdrawn or dismissed	Charges of which offenders were found guilty					(9) Charges not accounted for in cols (3)–(8)
			(4) Total findings of guilt	(5) Absolute discharge	(6) Conditional discharge	(7) Dealt with by fine	(8) Otherwise disposed of	
Emission of smoke, etc, causing danger: reg. 83, M.V.(C.&U.) regs., 1966	777	21	754	22	4	728	–	2
Noise caused by faulty silencer: ibid., regs. 21 and 81	12,533	326	12,141	166	66	11,888	21	66
Excessive noise due to defect or lack of repair or adjustment of load: ibid., reg. 86	439	24	414	8	1	405	–	1
Not stopping engine so far as necessary to prevent excessive noise when stationary: ibid., reg. 88	47	–	47	1	–	46	–	–
Sounding horn, in built-up area between 11.30 p.m. and 7 a.m., also when stationary: ibid., reg. 89	283	12	271	1	2	268	–	–
Excessive noise through lack of reasonable care by driver: ibid., reg. 87	376	22	354	3	6	345	–	–

Prosecutions and findings of guilt in 1969 for certain motoring offences relating to noise or pollution in England and Wales

(1) Offence	(2) Offences dealt with by prosecution	(3) Charges withdrawn or dismissed	Charges of which offenders were found guilty					(9) Charges not accounted for in cols (3)–(8)
			(4) Total findings of guilt	(5) Absolute discharge	(6) Conditional discharge	(7) Dealt with by fine	(8) Otherwise disposed of	
Emission of smoke, etc, causing danger: reg. 83 M.V. (C. and U.) regs., 1966	909	27	881	31	9	841	–	1
Noise caused by faulty silencer: Ibid., regs. 21 and 81	13,112	299	12,707	168	50	12,476	13	106
Excessive noise due to defect or lack of repair or adjustment of load: Ibid., reg. 86	359	21	338	2	2	334	–	–
Not stopping engine so far as necessary to prevent excessive noise when stationary: Ibid., reg. 88	55	1	54	–	–	54	–	–
Sounding horn in built-up area between 11.30 p.m. and 7 a.m., also when stationary: Ibid., reg. 89	244	11	232	6	–	226	–	1
Excessive noise through lack of reasonable care by driver: Ibid., reg. 87	247	7	238	1	2	233	2	2

Prosecutions and findings of guilt in 1970 for certain motoring offences relating to noise or pollution in England and Wales

(1) Offence	(2) Offences dealt with by prosecution	(3) Charges withdrawn or dismissed	Charges of which offenders were found guilty					(9) Charges not accounted for in cols (3)–(8)
			(4) Total findings of guilt	(5) Absolute discharge	(6) Conditional discharge	(7) Dealt with by fine	(8) Otherwise disposed of	
Emission of smoke, etc, causing danger: reg. 84, M.V. (C. and U.) regs., 1969	742	41	700	18	9	673	–	1
Noise caused by faulty silencer: Ibid., regs. 22 and 82	13,807	340	13,327	154	75	13,081	17	140
Excessive noise due to defect or lack of repair or adjustment of load: Ibid., reg. 87	241	11	227	1	1	225	–	3
Not stopping engine so far as necessary to prevent excessive noise when stationary: Ibid., reg. 90	43	1	42	–	–	42	–	–
Sounding horn in built-up area between 11.30 p.m. and 7 a.m., also when stationary: Ibid., reg. 91	292	7	285	3	1	280	1	–
Excessive noise through lack of reasonable care by driver: Ibid., reg. 88	228	20	204	–	1	203	–	4
Exceeding the maximum permitted sound level: Ibid., reg. 89	2	–	2	1	–	1	–	–

Appendix 3 Merchant Shipping (Oil Pollution) Act, 1971: commencement

Since the main text of this book went to press, sections of the Merchant Shipping (Oil Pollution) Act relating, *inter alia*, to liability for oil pollution damage have been brought into force.[1]

Section 1 provides that if an occurrence takes place while a ship is carrying a cargo of persistent oil in bulk resulting in the discharge or escape of persistent oil the owner of the ship shall be liable for

(*a*) damage caused in the area of the United Kingdom by contamination resulting from the discharge or escape; and

(*b*) the cost of any measures reasonably taken after the discharge or escape for the purpose of preventing or reducing such damage in the United Kingdom; and

(*c*) any damage caused in the area of the United Kingdom by any measures so taken.

Section 2 provides for the exceptions to liability agreed in the Convention,[2] and s. 3 provides that the owner shall not be liable otherwise than under the Act. The Act does not apply to warships or ships used by the government of any State for other than commercial purposes.[3]

1 Merchant Shipping (Oil Pollution) Act, 1971 (Commencement) Order, 1971.
2 See p. 92 *supra*, (*a*)–(*c*).
3 Section 14(1).

Index